Freeing Our Families from Perfectionism

Freeing Our Families from Perfectionism

Thomas S. Greenspon, Ph.D.

Edited by Pat Samples

free spirit
PUBLiSHiNG®

Works
for kids®

Library of Congress Cataloging-in-Publication Data
Greenspon, Thomas S., 1942–
    Freeing our families from perfectionism / by Thomas S. Greenspon.
        p. cm.
    Includes bibliographical references and index.
    ISBN 1-57542-103-8
    1. Perfectionism (Personality trait) 2. Perfectionism (Personality trait)—Case studies. 3. Child rearing. I. Title.

BF698.35.P47 G74 2002
155.2′32—dc21   2001040905

At the time of this book's publication, all facts and figures cited are the most current available; all telephone numbers, addresses, and Web site URLs are accurate and active; all publications, organizations, Web sites, and other resources exist as described in this book; and all have been verified. The author and Free Spirit Publishing make no warranty or guarantee concerning the information and materials given out by organizations or content found at Web sites, and we are not responsible for any changes that occur after this book's publication. If you find an error or believe that a resource listed here is not as described, please contact Free Spirit Publishing. Parents, teachers, and other adults: We strongly urge you to monitor children's use of the Internet.

Cover and book design by Marieka Heinlen
Index compiled by Randl Ockey

10 9 8 7 6 5 4 3 2 1
Printed in Canada

Free Spirit Publishing Inc.
217 Fifth Avenue North, Suite 200
Minneapolis, MN 55401-1299
(612) 338-2068
help4kids@freespirit.com
www.freespirit.com

Dedication

In fond memory of W. Haywood Burns and James Farmer, whose lives were devoted to the struggle for universal human acceptance.

Acknowledgments

A 1986 issue of the *Newsletter of the Minnesota Council for the Gifted and Talented* contained my first article about perfectionism, a subject that interested me professionally but for many years was also was my own Achilles heel. An early 1999 conversation with psychologist Maureen Neihart led to an invitation to contribute an article on this topic to a special issue of the *Journal for Secondary Gifted Education*, for which she was guest editor. The result was, "Healthy Perfectionism is an Oxymoron! Reflections on the Psychology of Perfectionism and the Sociology of Science," published in the summer of 2000. I'm indebted to Maureen for encouraging me to look more deeply into this topic and to begin writing about it again.

A little later my former student and longtime friend Judy Galbraith, founder and president of Free Spirit Publishing, approached me about writing a book for parents to complement Miriam Adderholdt's now classic *Perfectionism: What's Bad About Being Too Good?* Judy's highly enthusiastic support for my outlook on this subject has been extremely encouraging. Her exceptionally competent editorial staff has respectfully made it clear that there are helpful and less helpful ways of saying things, and that the harsher remnants of my own perfectionism would have to go if I expected the book to be in print.

This is a book for parents, teachers, and anyone in the general public with an interest in the topic of perfectionism. It's meant to be jargon-free, but I do want to note for my professional colleagues that the book is based on contemporary contextualist and intersubjective systems theories. I have written and spoken about this elsewhere.

The ideas central to this book have been shaped by many people:

My graduate school guru, Charles W. Eriksen, taught me that what someone says doesn't necessarily tell us what they are perceiving. Erik also imparted his curmudgeonly insistence on asking more questions before arriving at conclusions.

The widely-respected Adlerian psychotherapists Bill and Mim Pew invited me into their practice for a time many years ago, and gave me a solid grounding in the life-affirming encouragement process.

My supervisor and later colleague Ann Stefanson helped make empathy a central part of the work I do.

My therapist and spiritual guide Patrick Dougherty helped me to experience the retreat of perfectionism in the dawn of self-esteem.

Special thanks to my editor, Pat Samples, who is a true gem. In an incredibly intense and incredibly brief period of time, she helped me disassemble my original manuscript and reassemble it in what I hope is a helpful, readable, interesting way, exactly as I would have said it if I had known how. Knowing that Pat is an author herself, I found that her enthusiasm for this book gave me hope when the tasks seemed overwhelming.

My daughter and son-in-law Erin and David Holker, my son David, and his partner Kay Mickelson have seen my perfectionism up close. Their incisive humor and profound encouragement have sustained my excitement about the project. A little one, on its way but not here yet, has buoyed my hopes immensely. Thanks, "q"!

My clients in psychotherapy have always been both a source of data and a profound inspiration to me. I am in awe of the immense courage they show when they look inward, and of the vitalizing joy they discover as their connections deepen with partners and family.

Finally, every single point of view and suggestion for action in this book is the result of a 38-year-long professional and personal dialogue with my wife, Barbara. She is my partner and soul mate. This book is about the power of human connections, and Barbara has long been a shining example of passionate, empathic, supportive involvement in the lives of others. I worked on the manuscript for this book during our summer vacation two years running; I promise you, honey, next year we'll actually get out into Potagannissing Bay. It will be perfect.

Contents

Introduction

What's Wrong with Perfectionism?

Does your child or teen . . .

- seem highly competitive and constantly compare himself to others?

- find it hard to relax and enjoy the present moment?

- hesitate to take risks for fear of failing?

- experience frequent stress and anxiety?

- seem prone to discouragement?

- procrastinate often because of a need to do things perfectly?

- have difficulty in relationships because he expects too much of himself, or of others?

- appear to be a compulsive planner?

If you've noticed any of these tendencies, your child or teenager may be a perfectionist. None of them alone is a sure sign, but the more of them you've noticed, the more likely perfectionism is at work.

A perfectionist is someone who sets unrealistic goals and then feels extremely frustrated when the goals can't be met. Perfectionism can be seen at any age, even in very young children. It manifests itself in many ways, making it a challenge to combat. All the more reason to learn as much as you can about it.

Help for Your Child—and for You

Chances are, you're reading this book because you want help in dealing with your child's perfectionist ways of thinking and behaving. You don't want your child to be limited and frustrated by them. And frankly, your child's perfectionism may be driving you crazy.

You may also be wondering if you or others in your family have perfectionist tendencies that fuel those of your child. If so, reread the list on page 1 and see if any of these tendencies apply to you or to other adults in your household or family. If the answer is yes, then this book may be even more helpful than you had hoped. You will not only learn a new approach to your child's perfectionism, you will also learn new ways of handling perfectionist tendencies in yourself and other important people in your family life. Whether or not you are a perfectionist, this book is about changing how you and your child relate to one another, so it involves everyone in the family.

If your family is affected by perfectionism, it makes sense that you would want to make some changes, because perfectionism is painful. Perfectionists suffer greatly from their own self-criticism, and even if they do well at something, they can't enjoy it because they feel they should have done better. Intimacy seems elusive, because perfectionists avoid the vulnerability and risk-taking that intimacy requires. Work becomes overwhelming, because everything has to be done just right. Creativity slows to a trickle. Physical exhaustion is common, and there is little "juice" in life. Their high expectations, procrastination, and critical tendencies make everyone around them ill at ease.

No wonder you want to make changes.

I'm glad you're taking the time to read these pages and think about ways to get out from under the burden of perfectionism, whether you see it in your child, yourself, or other family members. Your interest in working on this means that your children and your family life are important to you, and that's the cornerstone of the plan I'll be showing you for overcoming perfectionism.

You're in Good Company

Perfectionism is a concern for many people. Whenever I speak publicly on any topic related to parenting or relationships, people in the audience are always eager to talk about their experience with perfectionism. No one can say just how widespread perfectionism is, partly because there are several ways to define it, but we do know that the modern winner-take-all attitude of our culture encourages it.

I've been a psychologist and marriage and family therapist for more than 30 years, and perfectionism has always interested me. I've read, written, and lectured widely on the subject, and I've helped many clients free themselves from perfectionism. In this book, I'll pass along to you what I've learned about perfectionism and how to overcome it. In doing so, I'll draw on not only my professional experience but my personal insights as well.

My kids were pancake lovers, especially when the cakes were poured in the shapes of their initials. I often did the cooking. My own perfectionism made me something of a loner in the kitchen, since things had to be done a certain way.

One day, our daughter wanted to participate in the cooking. Fine with me, I thought. We could have a good time together. Quickly, though, I found myself getting nervous, and even angry. She was making a mess and doing lots of things "wrong." I soon realized that my pointed commentaries were spoiling the fun for both of us and decided it was best if I left the job totally in her hands. She proudly took it on and made delicious pancakes, but my perfectionism cost me the chance to cook with my child that day.

In this book, you'll find many stories like this one. Some are about me and my family, but most are about other people I've known, including clients, workshop attendees, friends, and relatives. The stories are real; names, and sometimes genders, have been changed in order to protect people's privacy. The stories serve to illustrate important points and are meant to do three things: 1) remind you of similar experiences in your own life, 2) show you that you are not alone, and 3) demonstrate that perfectionism can be overcome.

Make This Your Book

The most important stories in these pages are yours. Throughout the book, you'll find invitations to "Make a Note of It." These are places where I give you ways to notice and reflect on your own experiences with perfectionism in your family. Use a notebook to jot down examples of what you observe. I'll give you lots of hints that will help you know what to look for. By using your own observations, you can tailor the book to your own situation and needs.

The notes can be anything from one-word reminders to lengthy journal entries. They are meant to help you see patterns that might be significant. You might even find it useful to make a note of other things going on at the time. For example, is your child's perfectionism more pronounced when she's tired, or has just been in an argument, or is feeling bad about something else that has happened?

A note of caution: You might be tempted to read your notes to your child or other family members as a way to point out their perfectionist traits, with the intention of letting them know what they are doing *wrong*. In reality, as you can imagine, this might only make them more self-critical or defensive. Instead, use your observations and note taking to help you become clearer about your concerns and get into a supportive conversation about what's going on.

You will also find invitations to "Talk It Over" throughout the book. These invitations consist of questions and activities to help you start conversations about perfectionism with your child and your whole family. Talk between family members is a powerful way to understand more about one another, and to build stronger family bonds. I recommend that you start talking with your family members as soon as you read the "Talk It Over" suggestions, and continue the conversations over time. They will naturally evolve as each person contributes, gains insights, and makes changes.

When having these dialogues with family members, make sure they observe your genuine involvement and curiosity—make eye contact, stay engaged, and be supportive. As you speak with your perfectionist child, you'll have a great opportunity to get inside her world. Attempting to understand your child's vantage point will bring two benefits at once: you'll get important information about why she acts the way she does, and your interest in her world will feel good to her—she'll feel understood, cared about, and hopeful. The same will be true of other family members when you show interest in their viewpoints.

The "Talk It Over" activities in this book can be done with your partner or child, or with the whole family. You may want to talk some things over with only one child, especially if there's some rivalry between your children. For other discussions, it would be helpful if everyone in the family is involved and can be a part of examining how the family works and how it could work better. Some families have more than one perfectionist child, and each exhibits perfectionism differently. Use your judgment on how to proceed with the "Talk It Over" activities, keeping in mind that the ultimate goal is to have everyone involved at some time.

A tip about taking action: If a family conversation leads to a suggestion that you do something differently, adopt an experimental attitude. Agree to try it for a week or two (depending on what seems appropriate), and then plan to check in with each other to see how it went. If the change was helpful, continue it. If not, talk about other ideas you could try.

Getting to the Bottom of Perfectionism

As you read the chapters and do the activities, *Freeing Our Families from Perfectionism* will help you understand and minimize the perfectionism in your family. In Part 1, you'll explore what perfectionism is, what its root causes are, and how to recognize it. In Part 2, you'll discover how to help your child overcome perfectionism and, if necessary, how to overcome it in yourself. In some chapters, a "Read More About It" list offers recommendations for books and other resources that can help you learn more. You'll also find a checklist in Chapter 1 that you can photocopy for your own use and for other family members.

Throughout the book, I will often suggest that you take a look at your own thoughts, feelings, and behaviors, and at the role you might be playing in your child's perfectionism. The purpose of this self-observation is not for you to take on blame but to help you take a wider view of the ways perfectionism may be present in your family so that you can respond to it more effectively. Since I have done this myself and have helped many other parents do so as well, I can tell you that it is worth the effort. In the end, your child will be free of a burden—and you will be free as well.

Families, Genders, and the Words We Use

This book is about children and their families, and families come in many forms. Yours may include biological or adoptive parents, step-parents, unmarried partners, or other significant adults living in your home or sharing in your family life in an important way. While no one word describes all these other adults that may be part of a family's life, I will mostly be using the word "partner" to do so, since each significant adult in your family life is in some way a partner in help-ing to shape your child's experiences. Feel free to substitute another word if it fits your family situation better or to ignore it if you don't have any partners in parenting.

When we're speaking about one person, no English pronoun covers both sexes. In this book, I'll alternate between using *she/her* and *he/his* in order to make it easier for you to relate to what you're reading, regardless of the sex of your child or partner.

The most important word in this book may be *hope.* That's what it offers, because if you're willing to learn, observe, and talk with your family about perfectionism, you can begin to free yourself from it and have a more satisfying and enjoyable family life. Best wishes on your journey!

> *True perfection exists only in obituaries and eulogies.*
> —ASHER PACHT

PART 1

Chapter 1

Recognizing Perfectionism

We all like to do things well, and we sometimes work for perfection on things that interest us greatly. But does that make us perfectionists? Where do people cross the line from the normal desire to do things well into the perfectionist behavior that leads to frustration for them and for those who love them? And how can we recognize and respond to perfectionism if it's present in our families?

Perfectionism isn't easy to define, although we might think we know it when we see it. But do we? Some things are dead give-aways—always having to line things up perfectly straight or showing extreme disappointment at anything less than an A. But other evidence may be more subtle, such as giving up on something if the first attempt fails or having difficulty making choices.

How can you tell if your child or your partner is a perfectionist? How do you know if *you* are? These are the questions you'll explore in this chapter. If you already know that this is an issue, this chapter will provide a helpful review.

What Is Meant by Perfectionism?

Just what *is* perfectionism, and what are its characteristics? Let's look first at the traits that make up perfectionism. Exploring these traits at the start will bring us to a satisfying definition, one that describes not so much what perfectionists do, but what goes on inside their minds. To make it simpler to recognize these traits, I've divided them into categories, but as you probably know from experience, perfectionism is anything but simple. In the end, you may not find the perfect definition. If that bothers you, be sure to read on—this is the book for you.

What Does Perfectionism Look and Sound Like?

The "Perfectionism at a Glance" list on pages 9–10 shows the range of ways that perfectionism is often expressed. Use it to help you identify where perfectionism exists in your family. Take a few moments and complete the checklist for your child, your partner, and yourself. You can photocopy the page and use it for other family members as well. The more of these items you check for someone, the more likely that person is a perfectionist.

Some traits may be present only part of the time, or present to a greater or lesser degree. Perfectionism can be mild, moderate, or extreme, and people can be perfectionists about some things and not about others.

The point is, wherever perfectionism shows up, and however strong it is, it interferes with one's peace of mind, and even one's ability to perform.

In her 1999 commencement speech at Mount Holyoke College, author Anna Quindlen spoke of overcoming her own perfectionism, a process she likened to laying down a "backpack full of bricks." She pointed out that being perfect requires an ability to imitate whatever the crowd or the times require, and to be the best at it. Then she said that ". . . nothing important, or meaningful, or beautiful, or interesting, or great ever came out of imitations. The thing that is really hard, and really amazing, is giving up on being perfect and beginning the work of becoming yourself."

Perfectionism at a Glance

1. Check the statements that apply to your child.

2. Check those that apply to your partner (spouse or other family adult).

3. Check those that apply to you.

How a Perfectionist Acts

	YOUR CHILD	YOUR PARTNER	YOU
Overcommits himself			
Rarely delegates work to others			
Has a hard time making choices			
Always has to be in control			
Competes fiercely			
Arrives late because one more thing had to be done			
Always does last-minute cramming			
Gets carried away with the details			
Never seems satisfied with his work			
Constantly busies himself with something or other			
Frequently criticizes others			
Refuses to hear criticism of himself			
Pays more attention to negative than positive comments			
Checks up on other people's work			
Calls himself "stupid" when he does something imperfectly			
Procrastinates			

What a Perfectionist Thinks

	YOUR CHILD	YOUR PARTNER	YOU
If I can't do it perfectly, what's the point?			
I should excel at everything I do.			
I always have to stay ahead of others.			
I should finish a job before doing anything else.			

continued →

Perfectionism at a Glance continued

	YOUR CHILD	YOUR PARTNER	YOU
Every detail of a job should be perfect.			
Things should be done right the first time.			
There is only one right way to do things.			
I'm a wonderful person if I do well; I'm a lousy person if I do poorly.			
I'm never good enough.			
I'm stupid.			
I can't do anything right.			
I'm unlikable.			
I'd better not make a mistake here or people will think I'm not very . . . [smart, good, capable].			
If I goof up, something's wrong with me.			
People shouldn't criticize me.			
Everything should be clearly black or white. Grays are a sign of confused thinking.			

How a Perfectionist Feels

	YOUR CHILD	YOUR PARTNER	YOU
Deeply embarrassed about mistakes she makes			
Disgusted or angry with herself when she is criticized			
Anxious when stating her opinion to others			
Extremely worried about details			
Angry if her routine is interrupted			
Nervous when things around her are messy			
Fearful or anxious a lot of the time			
Exhausted and unable to relax			
Plagued by self-hatred			
Afraid of appearing stupid			
Afraid of appearing incompetent			
Afraid of being rejected			
Ashamed of having fears			
Discouraged			
Guilty about letting others down			

The Many Faces of Perfectionism

One way to understand perfectionism better is to group its characteristics into behaviors, thoughts, and feelings. Behaviors refer to what we do—our actions, what people see as they watch us. Thoughts are the beliefs and ideas we have in our heads—little inner conversations we have with ourselves as we try to figure things out. Feelings are the stuff of our emotional life—fear, joy, anxiety, and anger, for example.

Some characteristics show up in all three categories on the "Perfectionism at a Glance" list, but in a slightly different form. For example, a person may think every detail must be perfect (thought), feel anxious or worried about the details (feeling), and get carried away with attention to details (action). All three forms carry a similar message, but each one gives you a different way to recognize it. The more windows you can look through as you examine how perfectionism shows up, the easier it will be to recognize it in your family and discover how to make changes for the better.

How Perfectionists Act

John is a worrywart. In school, he takes every assignment seriously and sets out to do it absolutely perfectly. He makes sure to do all the required reading and worries when he can't recall every main point without looking at notes. Should he read the material again? When he writes, will he remember to cover everything? Is there something he should know that may not *have been in the readings, that* should *be in his paper?*

John is in a flurry of activity prior to writing—gathering information sources, setting things up, arranging an outline, organizing his desktop. If you were watching him, you might begin to wonder if he was ever actually going to start *writing. When he does at long last, he appears to be in great distress about the first few sentences, each of which he rewrites several times.*

Sara is typically late with her assignments in school, and some of them never get done at all. Her parents describe her as lazy. They have set up regular study times for her in an attempt to help her get organized. While she complies by going to her room, she does so with a sullen face and big sigh. Then she sits at her desk and daydreams or does practically anything but study. Her grades have fallen, her teachers are concerned, and her parents are angry and desperate.

Is Agitated Overactivity Typical?

Many people would describe John as the typical perfectionist. He seems to be in constant turmoil, always doing something, never satisfied. For John, less-than-perfect results mean redoing the job. He's likely to say, "I'm such a dummy!" or "How could I be so stupid?" This chronic busyness, anxious manner, and self-critical commentary represent the most familiar forms of perfectionist behavior.

But what about Sara? She appears to be just the opposite: she doesn't seem to care how things turn out and is willing to just let things go.

If you're surprised to learn that Sara is also a perfectionist, then you're not alone. Sara's case shows us that the usual description of the typical perfectionist is limited, and that, in fact, perfectionism has more than one face. Perfectionists like Sara appear passive and disinterested and seem to give up in discouragement. Parents think that children like Sara are lazy or don't care. However, unlike Sara, kids who really don't care whether they succeed are rarely bothered by underperformance. Perfectionists like Sara, on the other hand, will typically seem distant, sad, depressed, or somewhat hostile when not performing well. They're thinking, "Since I can't seem to do it perfectly, what's the use?" To label them lazy misses the point.

So when it come to behaviors, perfectionists can range all the way from overdriven, anxious achievers to laconic, discouraged nonachievers.

Procrastination

All types of perfectionists can be serious procrastinators. People put things off for a number of reasons, but perfectionism is one of the more common ones. It's as if the perfectionist procrastinator says (usually unconsciously), "I might not do this job perfectly, so I'm not sure I want to do it at all." People who procrastinate to avoid imperfection are fearful and anxious, rather than lacking in motivation. Although a parent may interpret a child's procrastination at homework as laziness or even defiance, the perfectionist child is actually hesitating for fear of getting a less-than-perfect grade.

Telling the difference is not always easy, but a parent who sees other evidence of perfectionism might well suspect that fear is the motive when a child procrastinates.

Being Critical of Other People

My reluctance to let my daughter do the pancake-making tasks by herself, which I described in the introduction, was a form of perfectionist behavior. For whatever reason, it was a job I felt had to be done correctly, and that meant I had to do it. This insistence on doing it right is why perfectionists can be hard on other people. There are any number of ways this behavior can show up:

- Although a young man was accepted by a very fine college, his father said, "Well, it will do, but it isn't the Ivy League."

- A woman who is both a very successful entrepreneur and a good cook continues to receive coffee-making instructions whenever her watchful mother comes to visit.

- When a preschooler comes to his mother very excited about a drawing of a cat he has just made, she says, "Where's the tail?"

Make a Note of It

Take a closer look at the behaviors ("How a Perfectionist Acts") on the "Perfectionism at a Glance" list on page 9. In the next few days, jot down examples of these behaviors when you notice them in any family member. Be discreet so that no one feels spied on.

Talk It Over

Discuss with your child or partner some of the things in your notebook that concern you. Your main goal at first is to do some scouting—to gather information from the other person about how he perceives what's going on. Your family may be used to talking about personal subjects together; if not, here are some things that may help you:

First and foremost, although you may be angry about your child's behavior, angry confrontations will make resolving the problem harder. If, like most parents, you are mainly worried about your child (even if you're also angry), start from there. You might say, "I've been concerned about something for a while, and I've just realized it's that I'm sad about how you seem to struggle so hard at the last minute before a test. Does that bother you, too? Do you have any ideas about why that happens so often?" It's important to keep the focus not on the troublesome behavior, but on the internal struggle that seems to be going on when the child is behaving this way. Of course you may want your child to be less controlling, but the primary concern is how anxious he gets when he feels things are out of control.

If the behavior in question is something you do yourself, talk about this and suggest working together to change things. You might say, "I've been reading this book, and I can see something that both you and I seem to do . . . [name it]. Have you thought about that, too? Do you have any ideas about why we do it?" Bank on the fact that you and your child aren't the only ones who have this problem. If it's appropriate, you might say, "A friend of mine was telling me the other day that her son never seems to be satisfied with his schoolwork, even though he does very well. I realized that's something I've seen with you, too, and I wonder if that's a problem for you."

What if you get an exasperating shoulder shrug and "I dunno" for a response? Try the door-opener approach: say to your child, "Well, I'm interested in talking more about this, so I'd like both of us to think about it a bit. Let's talk about it in a few days." Then let it go, and come back to it in a few days—and keep trying.

If something is so important it *has* to be discussed, give choices, not about whether to talk but about who to talk with: "Would it be easier to talk to me or your dad [or a relative, trusted adult, counselor, clergy member, etc.] about this?"

Remember to keep your sense of humor in all of this. You might want to say, "I know details just drive me nuts! How about you?"

One more point: Ask questions when things are going well, not in the middle of an argument. In Part 2, you'll find more ideas on what you can do and say to make these conversations helpful.

What Perfectionists Think

Ray is a successful businessman who comes from a chaotic, alcoholic family in which there was physical and emotional abuse. He says he feels like a circus performer who keeps several plates spinning on the tops of long poles. Ray is always on top of everything—clients, customers, family activities, friends, hobbies—trying to make sure everyone is happy. As a child, he learned that if he struggled to make everything go well, his father might not be quite as angry. Though it rarely worked, Ray came to believe that trying to make things go perfectly would reduce the chaos and lead to harmony. Ray could be happy, he thought, if he could make everyone else happy.

■ ■ ■

Joan's parents believed that the way to help people grow was to point out their shortcomings so they could be aware of them and learn to do better. As a result, Joan heard only what she had done wrong, never what she had done well. From her parents' reactions, she concluded that she was never good enough. She didn't give up, though; Joan struggled to be perfect, in the hope that her mom and dad would finally be proud of her. Joan thought that if she could be perfect, she would be loved.

We all live by a set of convictions about who we are and what our role is in relationship to others. We frequently experience these convictions as a set of internal messages, or self-talk, which the examples above illustrate. Ray's belief is, "If I'm perfect, then my world can be peaceful, harmonious." For Joan, the belief is, "If I'm perfect, I can matter to people and be acceptable (lovable)."

Even though Ray and Joan have little evidence to support their beliefs, they keep struggling to be perfect, hoping to gain the love and harmony they desire. Their belief systems are deeply rooted in the environments in which they grew up, and they've been shaped by the interactions they had back then with significant adults in their lives.

The internal self-talk of most perfectionists shows something about the nature of perfectionism in general. Rarely do these messages have a positive, enthusiastic quality to them, such as "It would be really great to do this perfectly" or "I'd love to do a perfect job here." Instead, the self-talk has overtones of anxiety and demand, and the words *should, must, need to,* or *have to* are prominent: "I need to get a perfect score on this project" or "I have to win this one." This pressure, this necessity to do a perfect job, is a hallmark of perfectionism. Fear of making any mistake at all is common.

The internal self-talk of perfectionists typically involves a set of instructions about how they must act ("get a perfect score") or a statement about how well they're doing in life ("I never seem to get anything right"). If we asked them why they had to act in these ways or what they achieved by doing better, we'd probably find that it had to do with a desire to be acceptable to others.

Thinking Like a Perfectionist

- A man calls something by the wrong name in a conversation. Later, when he realizes his mistake, he says to himself, "I'm such an idiot!"

- A brilliant young student and athlete ignores several great plays she makes on the basketball court because of her belief that the one play she messed up was the single most important one and that this shows she is a poor player.

- A student concludes that she is no longer as bright as she used to be because she has received a lower grade than usual.

Make a Note of It

Take another look at the "Perfectionism at a Glance" list. This time, turn your attention to the items listed under "What a Perfectionist Thinks" (pages 9–10). Over the next few days, jot down any thoughts like these that you find yourself thinking.

Talk It Over

Have a conversation with your child and your partner in which you ask whether they often have the kind of thoughts described in the list, or other thoughts you may be wondering about. Use the same guidelines as in the last "Talk It Over" section (pages 13–14). Remember, none of us can read minds, so even though it may seem that your child is thinking a certain way, he may or may not be. In the spirit of exploration, ask—and be ready to hear a different answer than the one you expected. When you notice your child struggling endlessly with a project, you might ask, "Knowing that you work so hard on things, I wonder if you think every single detail of a job has to be perfect in order for it to be okay?" After your partner makes a mistake, ask, "When I see the way you look after something goes wrong, I wonder if you think making a mistake means something is wrong with you?" You can also share any of your own perfectionist thoughts.

Notice the use of the words "I wonder" in the questions above. Words like these show that you're genuinely curious about what your child or partner is thinking. Although you don't have to use that exact phrasing (it doesn't have to be perfect!), try to use language that shows you want to learn what your family members are thinking. "Could it be that you . . . " is another good opener.

Remember to listen as carefully as you can to what your family members say in response, so that you can get some clues about how they think. Remember, too, that their thoughts may be incorrect but that they're not irrational or laughable. If your child thinks he's never good enough, your job will be to help him feel better about himself, not to try to convince him that his thoughts are wrong.

What Perfectionists Feel

If internal self-talk draws the picture of perfectionism, emotions provide the color.

Sandy is a high schooler. She is a highly motivated student who always does exceptionally well. When Sandy is part of a small group project, she feels especially pressed to make sure that all the group members do their part, and do it well. Her fear of failure leads to her adamant insistence that everyone do things the "right" way, and to angry outbursts when they don't. Her fellow students have learned to steer clear of her at these times, and they frequently find her demanding ways to be irritating.

Fear, Anxiety, and Anger

Sandy's story illustrates the point that perfectionists can be as tough on others as on themselves. In many cases, this harshness toward others is the result of fear that someone else's poor performance will reflect badly on the perfectionist.

Fear is a powerful motivator; it mobilizes us to defend and protect ourselves. While moderate amounts of fear can help us, more intense fear, or fear that is chronic and more or less continuous, can actually have a devastating effect. This kind of fear robs us of our vitality as well as our ability to do well, and it causes us to do things we would otherwise judge irrational.

Fear can also lead to anxiety, especially when people have lived for a long time in chaotic or threatening situations. Some perfectionists experience a generalized state of anxiety, characterized by constant vigilance; they're afraid they'll do something wrong and are always watching for signs of disapproval.

Fear, general anxiety, and anger can all be part of the emotional landscape of perfectionism. Moderate fear of making mistakes can certainly lead to improved performance, but more intense, constant fear gets in our way and can lead to anger and a sense of powerlessness. Anger can interfere with performance, and with relationships as well. Powerlessness can paralyze us.

Shame

In many cases, what characterizes a person's perfectionism is something more profound and all-pervasive than fear: shame. Shame is not so much a single emotion as an overall sense of inferiority and unacceptability. It is a feeling of being judged and found lacking.

Jacob always feels it is important to be right, and to be completely knowledgeable about whatever his group happens to be discussing. This frequently means that he becomes angry and impatient in a discussion when people don't agree about something. When others have a different point of view from his, Jacob comes across as self-righteous, but inside he begins to feel his face burning—embarrassed over not knowing enough or not being able to get people to agree with him. He begins to secretly wonder if he isn't somehow inescapably flawed and not as bright as he thought he was.

It may be surprising that shame and embarrassment can be a part of perfectionism. Perfectionists are often thought of as arrogant and overdriven; their nagging feelings of inferiority or of never quite being good enough are well hidden from public view. However, although arrogance and grandiosity characterize many perfectionists, and although these qualities can cause problems in relationships, *they are not at the root of perfectionism.* Their perfectionism is not a form of showboating or demonstrating how good they are—rather, it is grounded in the fear that they are not good enough.

Perfectionists are also sometimes viewed in a positive way, as confident, ambitious, energetic, and competent. This effectively masks any shame they might feel, and any underlying feelings of inadequacy. It's easy to make the mistake of thinking that the perfectionism is responsible for these positive traits, when in reality perfectionism, like any anxiety people have about their performance, can actually get in the way of their ambition and success. That's because perfectionist anxieties tend to make us self-conscious and overly focused on how well we're doing, which interrupts the flow of a task. To get an idea of how this works, try carrying a full cup of coffee across a room. Looking directly at the liquid in the cup in order to avoid spilling it makes a spill more likely. The psychiatrist David Burns established in his research some years ago that highly accomplished people are less likely to be perfectionists. Those perfectionists who do become very successful in life still tend to feel the burden of their perfectionism.

Sometimes perfectionists are ashamed of their fears. Messages we all hear, such as "There's nothing to be afraid of" and "Don't be a baby," catch some perfectionists in an impossible bind: they worry about not being able to do something well enough, and they worry about worrying too much.

Make a Note of It

Look at the feelings listed in "Perfectionism at a Glance" on page 10. Ask yourself whether you experience any of these feelings with any regularity. Over a few days' time, notice when such feelings arise. Each time, ask yourself what happened in the last little while that might explain these feelings, and make a note of it.

Talk It Over

If you think other family members have these feelings, check that out with them. Ask. Try saying, "It seems like you're angry about something these days. Am I right about that?" Apply the same principles suggested in the first "Talk It Over" section (pages 13–14). Talking about feelings will be easiest if you can empathize—listen carefully to what your child and partner say, and accept what you hear, trying to put yourself in their place. It may not be the same way you would feel in the same circumstance, but use this opportunity to learn about what they're experiencing.

Their feelings may be based on incorrect thoughts, but your job is not to try to convince them that their feelings are wrong or crazy. Feelings are just feelings. They are what motivates people to do what they do. So it makes sense that, if your child is anxious about something, she might get very busy trying to make it come out right. Listen to her, acknowledge and confirm her feeling ("You're feeling a lot of pressure to get that done right, aren't you?"), and let her know you want to help her relieve that feeling. You'll find many ideas on how to do that in Part 2 of this book. For now, what's important is to listen, learn, and show you care.

Other Perspectives on Perfectionism

Behaviors, thoughts, and feelings provide one way to think about perfectionism. There are other ways as well. One group of researchers,[1] for example, identified three dimensions that describe perfectionism: the *self-oriented* (being hard on oneself), the *other-oriented* (being hard on others), and the *socially prescribed* (struggling to meet standards set by others).

Another group of researchers developed a Multidimensional Perfectionism Scale by examining the results of questionnaires given to large groups of people.[2] This scale identifies such elements of perfectionism as high personal standards, the perception of high parental expectations and high parental criticism, doubting the quality of one's actions, and a preference for order and organization. But the major characteristic these researchers found was concern over mistakes. This is a very important point. *It is concern over mistakes, rather than pride of accomplishment, that most accurately characterizes perfectionism.*

Perfectionism is not pleasurable. It isn't a badge of honor, and those who feel proud of it are typically confusing their talents and capabilities with their perfectionism. In fact, perfectionism interferes with a person's ability to do well.

---

[1] Hewitt, P. L. & Flett, G. L. (1991). "Perfectionism in the Self and Social Contexts: Conceptualization, Assessment, and Association with Psychopathology," *Journal of Personality and Social Psychology,* Volume 60, Number 3, 456–470.
[2] Frost, R. O., et al. (1990). "The Dimensions of Perfectionism," *Cognitive Therapy and Research,* Volume 14, Number 5, 449–468.

Perfectionism does not determine success.
Talent, energy, and commitment do.

For perfectionists, critical self-judgment looms large. Perfectionists fear failure more than they desire success. This is why perfectionism is painful, and why it is not the same as healthy striving to reach high goals. At its core, perfectionism is a no-win approach to life. If perfectionists make mistakes, their self-criticism is harsh. Yet if they do well, they can't bask in the glow of good feelings, since any job could always have been done better.

Healthy Perfectionism?

Some people say there is a *healthy* perfectionism. However, it's important to distinguish between having the talent, energy, and commitment to do well—maybe even do a particular thing perfectly—and perfectionism. Perfectionism is a desire or need, not just to do well, but to be perfect. Research and clinical experience have shown repeatedly that perfectionism is more about the fear of failure than the urge for success, and that it gets in your way. Perfectionism is never healthy. At times, a burning desire to be perfect may help you get something you want, but that doesn't make it a healthy way to think or behave.

Perfectionists are successful despite *their*
perfectionism, not because *of it.*

Definition of Perfectionism

As you can see from what you've read so far, perfectionism isn't easy to define. But *Merriam-Webster's Medical Desk Dictionary* sums it up quite well:

> a disposition to regard anything short of perfection as unacceptable; *especially:* the setting of unrealistically demanding goals accompanied by a disposition to regard failure to achieve them as unacceptable and a sign of personal worthlessness.

Notice that the definition doesn't talk about a healthy striving for excellence. Trying your hardest, going all out, extending yourself beyond your usual limits, and even overdoing it are not perfectionist behaviors in themselves. Instead, as the definition says, perfectionists set *unrealistically* demanding goals, and when they fail to achieve these goals, they feel *unacceptable* and *personally worthless*.

> *Perfectionism and striving for excellence*
> *are not the same thing.*

The Impossible Dream

Perfection is an impossible goal. We're not perfectible, and it will only be occasionally possible to do things perfectly, if it's possible at all.

> *No good work whatever can be perfect, and the demand for perfection*
> *is always a misunderstanding of the ends of art.*
> —JOHN RUSKIN

We will all make mistakes, goof up, do things we shouldn't, and fail to do things we should. This will always be human nature. Instead of beating ourselves up over mistakes, we can simply go ahead and do what is needed in the situation, including fixing our mistakes if that's possible. It's better to try something and learn from our mistakes than to hesitate out of worry and miss an opportunity for accomplishment. The only way never to make a mistake is never to do anything.

> *. . . this mistaken idea of the importance of mistakes leads us*
> *to a mistaken concept of ourselves. We become overly impressed*
> *by everything that is wrong in us and around us. . . .*
> *To be human does not mean to be right, does not mean to be perfect.*
> *To be human means to be useful, to make contributions—*
> *not for oneself, but for others—to take what there is*
> *and make the best out of it.*
> —RUDOLF DREIKURS

What's Next?

In the next chapter, you'll discover how a mistake becomes something more than just a mistake—how it seems to become evidence of a character flaw. In Part 2, you'll learn how the perfectionists in your family can turn mistakes back into nothing more than mistakes instead of using them as proof of their failure as human beings.

 Read More About It

The Gifted Kids' Survival Guide: A Teen Handbook by Judy Galbraith and Jim Delisle (Minneapolis: Free Spirit Publishing, 1996). This is by far the best and most readable collection of information and self-help suggestions for kids and parents alike on a broad range of topics, including perfectionism.

Perfectionism: What's Bad About Being Too Good? by Miriam Adderholdt and Jan Goldberg (Minneapolis: Free Spirit Publishing, 1999). This useful and highly readable book on how to deal with perfectionism and how to distinguish it from a healthy striving for excellence was written for teenagers, but parents will appreciate it, too.

Too Perfect: When Being in Control Gets Out of Control by Allan E. Mallinger and Jeannette DeWyze (New York: Clarkson Potter, 1992). This book shows how perfectionism can sap energy, complicate simple decisions, and take the enjoyment out of life. It provides self-tests, case histories, and practical strategies to help overcome obsessiveness and reclaim a saner, healthier life.

Online University Counseling Center Brochures

For a quick look at some basic ideas about perfectionism, check out these Web sites sponsored by student counseling centers at major American universities.

Perfectionism
Counseling Center, University of Illinois at Champaign-Urbana
www.couns.uiuc.edu/Brochures/perfecti.htm

Perfectionism: A Double-Edged Sword
Counseling and Mental Health Center, University of Texas at Austin
www.utexas.edu/student/cmhc/perfect.html

Chapter 2

How Do We Become Perfectionists?

Now that you have a basic idea of what perfectionism is and how to recognize it, it's logical to ask: Where does perfectionism come from? How did my child become so concerned with being perfect? Understanding the origins of perfectionism will make it easier to figure out what you and your child can work on changing.

Your child's perfectionism didn't appear suddenly out of nowhere, and there's no one incident that caused it. It's the result of your child's ongoing interactions with the people around him, including you. In psychological terms, perfectionism is *relational*. This means that someone in addition to your child is involved in creating it. Perfectionists have an underlying fear that they won't be acceptable to someone if they don't do well enough. They're constantly trying to excel in order to win the approval and love of other people. Think about your child for a moment. Do you have any notion whose love and approval he might be seeking?

Although it may at first be disheartening to realize that you and others in the family have a role in your child's perfectionism, it's actually good news. It means that each of you can also play a role in overcoming it. Surprisingly few elements of your child's personality are completely unchangeable, especially if he feels understood and hopeful. You too can change, regardless of your age, so if you have perfectionist tendencies, the information and suggestions in this book can offer help and hope for both you and your child.

Criticism Versus Support

Compare the following two scenarios:

Jason rushes into the house with a picture he drew in his second-grade art class. He shows it to his dad, who says, "Okay, but what's this: does a person really look this way, with his arms at that angle? And you need to liven up the background, use more colors. What did the teacher say about this?" Jason takes the picture to his room, tears it into little pieces, and throws it at the wastebasket.

Kyle, a child from the same class, also waves his art project at his dad. "Awriiight!" says Kyle's dad. "Looks like you had fun in school today." "Yeah, it was great," says Kyle. "But my picture's kind of boring. I wish I could figure out how to make it look better." His dad responds, "Well, let's take a look. Maybe the two of us can come up with some ideas about that."

These two stories illustrate an important point about perfectionism, and about psychological development in general. What we think of our accomplishments, and what we think of ourselves as people, depends heavily on what we hear from people who matter to us. Perfectionism is an attempt to be more acceptable to others.

Let's assume these scenes are typical for Jason and Kyle in their homes. In Jason's case, his excitement about what he's done is routinely met with judgments about the quality of his work and comments about how he should have done it. Can you imagine what Jason eventually will conclude as a result of these comments? No matter how well-meaning his dad is, Jason may well come to believe that his work is never good enough and that his enthusiasm is misplaced. Jason's attempts to feel more acceptable and less defective may end up as perfectionism.

Kyle, on the other hand, finds his excitement mirrored by his father, who seems genuinely happy that his son likes doing his art activities. When Kyle himself expresses some dissatisfaction with his accomplishments, his dad seems to believe that dissatisfaction is a normal part of learning, that Kyle can certainly improve if he wants to. Kyle's father is willing to help him get better. Can't you imagine Kyle's feeling of accomplishment and his excitement about being able to improve? The sense that the important people in your life believe in you and accept you is the basis for self-acceptance.

Kyle could easily be on his way to self-improvement without also being on his way to perfectionism. Sadly, the opposite may be true for Jason. Two different kinds of relationships, two different outcomes.

Make a Note of It

How was it when you were growing up? Was your home atmosphere more like Jason's or Kyle's? What did your parents say when you were proud of something? When you were discouraged? Jot down your recollections.

What about your reactions to your children? Are you more like Jason's dad or Kyle's? What do you or your partner do when your child is proud of herself? What about when she is discouraged about something? Watch for instances of pride or discouragement in your child over the next few days and note how you respond to her. Jot down what you do and say. Do your reactions remind you of how your parents treated you when you were growing up? If so, think about how you felt and what you concluded about yourself. Do you notice your child having reactions that are similar reactions to yours?

Remember: the goal is to identify patterns of behavior now so that as you continue to read, you'll know how to change the way you react.

Psychological Origins

Human psychology can help us understand where perfectionism comes from. Let's start by considering two basic elements of our psychological makeup: emotional convictions and human connections.

Emotional Convictions

Every second of every day, from the moment we are born and without realizing it, we are actively making sense out of our world. We fit everything we see, hear, touch, taste, and smell into some kind of a meaningful whole, which is our experience of the world—the thing we call reality. A part of this reality is the continuous sense of I or me, the person who has the experience. Surprisingly—and this is a very important point to remember as you read this book—much of this sense of ourselves and of the meaning we give to our experiences depends on the kinds of relationships we have with others. Over the last 30 years, numerous studies of human development have demonstrated this. Even if Jason and Kyle had somehow drawn exactly the same picture, it would mean something entirely different to the two boys. That's because the ongoing attitudes reflected in their dads' different reactions to the pictures would lead the boys to different experiences of themselves. As we're growing up, significant relationships we have with others lead us to a set of expectations that help shape our experience. Donna Orange, a psychologist who has written extensively about this subject, calls these expectations *emotional convictions.* What we make of any encounter depends heavily on these emotional convictions.

Human Connections

All our experiences take place within a web of relationships with others. We actually need this web in order to be fully human. Research repeatedly shows that social isolation eventually leads to mental and emotional breakdown. For example, infants who are deprived of social contact, even if they are fed well, may not survive. We need relationships for our physical and emotional health, and we need them in order to maintain a sense of meaning in our world and a sense of who we are.

Making Sense Together

To put it simply, we're always making sense of our world, and we're always trying to maintain connections with others. These two elements of our humanity constantly affect one another: our understanding of things affects how we act with others, and our relationships with others affect our emotional convictions. What sense we make of the world, we make together.

Perfectionism reflects the particular meaning that perfectionists give to their relationships. If Jason is on his way to perfectionism, it's because his dad (and maybe other important adults as well) make it clear that Jason has to do better just to be accepted. Jason's need for connection with his dad gives his dad a powerful hand in developing Jason's emotional conviction that he is not okay as he is, and that he has to do better. By contrast, Kyle's dad implies that Kyle is lovable whatever his accomplishments might be; Kyle wants to improve, but he doesn't feel he has to in order to be accepted.

Self-Worth Defined by Others

This understanding of where perfectionism comes from explains why, in the dictionary definition on page 21, falling short of perfection seems unacceptable and a sign of personal worthlessness. To a perfectionist, being perfect looks like the only way to be worthwhile in the eyes of others.

But we don't become perfectionists only because of our parents' influence. We all live in a larger web of relationships as well. We are often confronted by cultural standards about behavior, dress, and accomplishment, not to mention about thoughts and feelings. Children may feel they have to wear a certain hairstyle or designer-label clothes in order to fit in. Adults are expected to look businesslike in certain settings, or to laugh at certain kinds of jokes. We sense strong judgments against us if we don't conform to certain norms. From an early age, your child learns that if he doesn't measure up to certain standards, he will be considered out of it, or defective. The prevailing winner-take-all attitude seems to tell us and our children: if you're not perfect, you're just a loser.

Acceptance

At the heart of your child's perfectionism is a concern about being accepted for who she is. As a parent, your job is not so much to figure out the correct way to eliminate perfectionism—after all, always having to do things correctly is often the problem in the first place. Rather, your task is to create a home environment where your child can count on feeling accepted and where cultural expectations are put into perspective, even if they are still adhered to.

The influence you have on your child is powerful, and it's not something you decide to have. It's a part of human nature, and unavoidable. Of course, you don't want this influence to be negative, and if it's been that way in the past, the good news is that you can change. You can decide to do things differently, and different results will follow. Imagine that you're Jason's dad. What would happen if you said, "Jason, I'm really sorry about what just happened. It's great to see you so excited about your art project, and I don't know why I had to be so critical. I hope you'll keep drawing"? Chances are that Jason's sense of his world—his emotional convictions—would begin to change.

What About Biology?

Although many perfectionist children have at least one perfectionist parent, it may never be possible to know how much the perfectionism is the result of genetic inheritance and how much is the result of environmental influences. Perfectionism isn't a basic temperament like assertiveness or avoidance. It's a highly complex phenomenon that only appears after a child has been living and growing in a certain environment. Whatever biological history a child has, his human environment is going to assert an influence from the moment of birth (if not before). Perfectionism is a complex pattern of behavior that takes time to develop. The later any behavioral pattern develops and the more complex it is, the more likely that a child's network of relationships played a major role in its development.

Could there be a medication for perfectionism? Probably not. Medications may help perfectionists who also happen to be depressed or highly anxious, but only because being less depressed or anxious makes it easier for them to work on their perfectionism.

The Many Wellsprings of Perfectionism

Jason's story on page 25 illustrates one way that perfectionism can develop in families: a child is frequently criticized, rarely affirmed, always told that he could do better. His desire to be accepted and loved by his father, and his emotional conviction that perfecting his work is the way to do this, leads to his perfectionism.

But direct criticism isn't the only way this happens.

Shannon sits down to dinner with her dad and mentions a problem she is having with one of her high school classmates. She is angry and sad about what has happened. Dad says: "Don't bother getting mad, just get even. You should tell that so-and-so. . . ." Shannon replies, unconvincingly, that she has already tried that approach. The conversation becomes a monologue by her dad, and Shannon finally leaves the table.

In some ways, Shannon's dad is like Jason's, except he isn't directly criticizing his daughter. In his mind, he's trying to be helpful, suggesting ways for her to solve the problem. But what Shannon is looking for is *emotional* support during this tough time with her friend, not *solutions*. She's a bright student who prides herself on solving problems and expects to figure things out for herself. But what she gets in the way of "help" from her dad is the message that she *can't* solve this problem on her own. She is also learning that only if she does things her dad's way will she have his love. Later in the book, you'll see that the problem for Shannon's dad is not that he didn't use the right words; it's that he didn't understand Shannon's perspective and therefore couldn't understand how she would hear his advice.

Here are more examples of family situations that gave rise to perfectionism:

- A young man remembers daily conversations between his parents in which they made derogatory statements about friends, neighbors, or relatives. He also remembers doing whatever he could to keep from becoming the object of such scorn.

- A woman remembers growing up with constant arguing and verbal sniping between her parents. They finally divorced when she was 15, but she had long since concluded that she was somehow responsible for their difficulties, and that she had to be a perfect little girl in order to try to keep them together.

- A man remembers his mother as very high-strung and perfectionistic. Everything had to be just so in the house, and he remembers feeling infected by her many issues about orderliness, so that he too had to have everything just right.

- A man remembers frequently hearing his father's tirades about "how lucky kids are today" and how "they don't know how good they have it." He remembers trying to prove his gratitude by doing everything just right.

The common thread in all of these stories about families of perfectionists is that, through the eyes of the perfectionist, gaining acceptance and harmony means having to do things *just right*.

The Dysfunctional Family

Families do not need to be chaotic or dysfunctional to produce perfectionists. Yet those qualities may contribute to their development. Many adult children of alcoholics, for example, can describe how their perfectionism came about.

Brian's dad could be very overbearing and controlling when he drank, which was most evenings and weekends. Brian and his mom and two sisters learned to either avoid dad or make pleasant conversation, which would not become controversial in any way. It didn't always work, though, and there were many times when his dad would be rageful and threatening. Brian remembers pouring all his energy into school and other interests away from home. He became a straight-A student, captain of the basketball team, and student body president, and he was involved in other community and church activities.

Brian remembers several reasons for this high drive to achieve: He was able to get out of the house and away from the conflict. He had things to focus on that made him feel good about himself. He never had time to dwell on the deep anger and sadness he felt about his family's problems. And he hoped that his dad would take so much pleasure in his achievements that he would find less to be angry about.

Whether family turmoil comes from chemical abuse, severe depression and suicidal threats, mental illness, abusive behavior, constant fighting, or the criminal activity of parents, it can produce perfectionism because of a child's desire to seek acceptance and safety amidst his troubled environment. Fueled by a strong but unrealistic hope that perfect performance will bring security, perfectionism itself can become like an addiction.

Neglect

A child's home environment doesn't have to include criticism or turmoil to create perfectionism. Parental neglect, constant preoccupation with something other than the life of the child, or chronic emotional coldness and formality can also drive a child to pursue perfection in order to find connection and acceptance.

A highly successful, perfectionistic woman remembers her father as a much-in-demand physician who, because of his total devotion to his patients and his work, was rarely at home. She remembers many times when he would leave in the middle of a family celebration to respond to an emergency call; he never mentioned his feelings about this, and never asked his children (or his wife) how they felt.

■ ■ ■

A man's parents were active card players who spent several nights a week out at card parties or tournaments. There were many get-togethers at home, but the adults were all playing cards and talking among themselves, and the children were frequently sent to their bedrooms early so they would not interfere. The man remembers as a child striving for perfect performance on the piano, so that his parents, who would often bring him out to play for the party, would include him in their activities.

Both of these people are struggling with perfectionism that sprang from a desire to become noticeable and important to their parents. Parental neglect and emotional detachment give children the message that they are not important. In some cases, children even feel invisible. Perfectionism is an attempt to say "I'm here—I'm important."

Giftedness

Many parents of gifted and talented children are concerned about perfectionism, but research thus far seems to indicate that gifted kids are no more prone to perfectionism than other kids. The families of gifted people sometimes do have characteristics that foster its development, though. Gifted kids who feel unacceptable may come to believe that their ability to do things like schoolwork perfectly offers a road to acceptance. In addition, the families of many gifted kids have one or more parents who are high achievers and demand much of themselves, and also of their children. When parents with these high expectations cross the line from encouraging full development and enjoying their child's gifts to insisting on perfection in all endeavors, then the seeds of perfectionism are sown.

Too Much Praise?

Can you praise your child too much? Could that lead to perfectionism?

One woman who struggles with perfectionism remembers constantly being told by her parents how good she was, and how she was the kind of person who could do anything she wanted to do. She remembers worrying a lot about whether she could continue to live up to this expectation. What would happen if she couldn't?

There is a difference between praise and encouragement. *Encouragement is focused on the enjoyment your child experiences when doing an activity. Praise is focused on the outcome of a task.* Since praise is usually greater for greater accomplishment, it often includes a subtle message that lower accomplishment is not good enough. When parents put too much emphasis on praise, using it as a reward for acceptable behavior, little allowance is made for having a bad day, being distracted, not feeling well, being bored, or having little interest in something—which are all normal parts of living. In Part 2, you'll learn more about the differences between praise and encouragement and how to use them as you help your child overcome perfectionism.

Make a Note of It

Would you describe the family you grew up in as dysfunctional? Neglectful? Having expectations that were too high? Jot down your recollections. If you're struggling with perfectionism, do you think your family history played a role?

Can you see any of these issues in your current family? Make a note of the times when you see yourself repeating old family patterns. Watch for such things as: expecting your child to get something perfect after only a few tries; staying too busy or otherwise being distant from her; having her show off her achievements to impress your friends; other actions that remind you of the pressures you felt as a child to prove yourself acceptable.

Please don't use these observations to criticize yourself or the family you came from. Rather, look for the patterns that might have led to any perfectionism that you developed over time. We can't change history, but we can change what will happen in the future by understanding more about what is going on now.

Talk It Over

Ask your partner to consider the same set of questions as in the "Make a Note of It" on page 33 and to make notes about them. Then compare notes, discussing with each other what you have learned about your individual family histories and your current tendencies to repeat old family patterns. Be honest about your own discoveries. Listen with interest, and without judgment, as your partner describes his. Stay away from criticism and don't try to change him. Instead, try to appreciate how difficult it is for your partner, as it may be for you, to realize that he is continuing to follow old family patterns that may be promoting perfectionism in your child. Thank him for being willing to discuss these subjects with you.

Conversations such as these, based in mutual respect and compassion, will make it easier for both of you to begin changing and to notice and support each other's efforts.

Different Children, Different Reactions

No set of circumstances is absolutely certain to produce perfectionism. You may recognize your family in one of the stories presented here and wonder why you are a perfectionist and your siblings are not, or vice versa. Each child experiences family life differently, and no two children are treated exactly alike. For example, in some families boys are given more recognition than girls. In such a family, one boy may coast while another works hard to prove that he's good for other reasons than simply being male. Meanwhile, one of the girls may struggle to do everything right, hoping to be accepted, while another gets discouraged and gives up. We can identify patterns of family interaction that lead to perfectionism, but we can't say what will necessarily happen in any particular case. In the end, it depends on how acceptable a child feels, and how that affects the particular child.

Mutual Influence

Not only do we influence our children's development, but our children also influence our behavior, and this reciprocal influence can intensify perfectionism. As parents, we have our own set of emotional convictions, and our own wishes for connection, including connection with our children. Our children in turn, respond to this as part of their own development.

Leah's mom was shy in school and always felt awkward and different. Leah was the kind of child who had only one or two close friends. Her mom began to worry that Leah was going to be like she was—too socially isolated—so she turned on the pressure for Leah to be more outgoing. Leah pushed herself to comply, but her discomfort only worried her mom more, which led to more pressure and then more discomfort on Leah's part, in an endless cycle.

Overcoming perfectionism always means changing things for each person in the family system. The decisions you make to do things differently will lead to changes in the whole system of relationships and will benefit everyone.

> *The blessed work of helping the world forward,*
> *happily does not wait to be done by perfect men.*
> —GEORGE ELIOT

What's Next?

How can you understand the world from your child's perspective? How can you create a family atmosphere of unconditional acceptance and love but still help your children learn and grow? That's what you'll explore in Part 2.

Chapter 3

Learning to Dive

As you read in Chapter 1, fear is common for perfectionists—fear of rejection and of feeling stupid, for example. In Part 2, you'll learn the different elements of a plan for freeing your family from perfectionism, including how to free your child from fears she has about her performance and acceptability to others.

Are You Feeling Any Fear?

You may be experiencing some fears of your own at this point, which prompt you to question whether there is any hope for your family: Will your child be able to overcome perfectionism? Will you be able to help? Will your partner participate? Are you part of the reason for your child's perfectionism? Is it too late to change?

Some people can dive right into a problematic situation—even a difficult one—and begin doing things in new ways. Others find this difficult because their fears paralyze them. If you're feeling hesitant and fearful about diving in, this chapter will help you find your courage.

As you learned in Chapter 1, a certain level of cautious concern is useful in keeping you aware of danger. Eliminating fear altogether is neither helpful nor even possible. Courage is not a state of fearlessness.

Courage is the ability to take action
despite our fears.

In the following pages, you'll learn ways to go about building or strengthening a home environment of acceptance and support. Such an environment is crucial to freeing your family from perfectionism and helping family members face and decrease their fears. I've been inspired by the sincerity and courage of the parents I've watched go through this process. In these pages, I hope you'll find lots of encouragement as you take on this important task.

Life shrinks or expands in proportion to one's courage.
—ANAÏS NIN

Take It Slow and Easy

Be patient with yourself as you practice the suggestions in the rest of this book. Give yourself all the time you need to learn how to do them. Some improvements may come soon, but it usually takes a while to overcome family habits. You may experience some confusion, and even feel resistance at first. Don't force the issue, but don't give up. The plan outlined in the following chapters is about developing an attitude rather than a set of techniques, so experiment with your approach, saying and doing the things I suggest in a way that feels comfortable to you. If you try something that lands with a thud, try something else. You're starting an ongoing process, and one advantage to that is that no one part has to be perfect. If it doesn't go well, you can redo it or do something different. Having the courage to accept your own mistakes is a great way to help your children accept theirs.

Don't Dive in Alone

The perfectionist in your family will find that working on the plan in Part 2 will be easier with the support of others. When perfectionists know that their fears and self-condemnation are not unique to them, and when they know they're acceptable to others just as they are, a profound healing can take place and they can do many things they didn't think were possible.

Working with your partner as you move forward is invaluable. You may have already started to do that in Part 1, but close collaboration and mutual support are even more important as you work on changing your home environment.

If you're a single parent, or if your partner isn't willing to join you in working on these changes, seek out a relative, a good friend, or a group you can talk with as you move forward. It will make your task much easier. If you can't think of anyone, check out parent education classes or parent support groups offered through your local Y, your health care provider or hospital, your child's day-care center, or a college or community education program. You can also check out support networks or resources for parents and families at your place of worship. If you are in recovery from addiction, Twelve Step groups such as Alcoholics Anonymous and Al-Anon can be a natural source of support. Find at least one person who can be a caring companion and source of encouragement on your journey of change.

Talk It Over

Have a talk with your partner or support person about any fears you have about this process. Facing fears together feels much better than facing them alone. Over time, discuss your other emotional reactions as you learn and apply the elements of the plan for freeing your family from perfectionism. You've already learned a little about how to talk with your partner in earlier chapters. Keep the process going. Check in with each other on a regular basis. In later chapters, you'll learn even more about the value of ongoing dialogue.

Begin your talks with whatever you're experiencing at the time. For example, "I guess this problem goes deeper than I thought. That's a little scary for me—what about you?" Or, "I'm getting nervous about trying this new stuff. I feel self-conscious. Do you ever feel that way?" If your partner hasn't read this book and answers, "No, I'm just fine," remember that your fears are still normal, and it's still okay to ask for support for yourself.

Easing Your Way Out of Perfectionism

When I first learned how to dive into the water off the dock at summer camp, my counselor was very patient. He told me to stand at the edge of the dock, hold my hands over my head, and let myself fall over headfirst into the water. I was a good swimmer already, and I had jumped into the water many times, but this was my first dive. I assumed the pose, bent at the waist to lean toward the water, and froze. I thought about it, I tried to imagine what was about to happen, then I tried *not* to imagine what was about to happen, then I tried to just close my eyes and fall over. Nothing. I walked away from the dock, then I came back. The counselor waited (he had other swimming area duties to attend to in the meantime). I was caught between wanting badly to be able to dive and being totally scared of doing it.

The counselor's ultimate solution was to find a way to hold on to me as I bent over so far that my hands were touching the water. Then he asked if I was ready, and when I finally said yes, he let go. I felt the explosion of sound and water all around me, and after a moment of confusion I came to the surface laughing. I was ecstatic. The counselor was applauding. The next few dives were on my own; I was still hesitant until I got used to diving, but then I felt totally free. Later in the week, I dove off the diving board, and later that summer I dove off of the high platform. What a summer.

This small success story may not describe the only way to overcome fears, but it was an instructive way. Notice that I was not alone. The counselor was willing to do whatever it took to help, and he was willing to wait for me to get my fears to a manageable level. He had nothing invested in my success; I could swim in the lake and go in a canoe even if I never learned how to dive. He was encouraging and supportive but not pushy, and he never ridiculed my fears or tried to talk me out of them. He set the stage for me to do what I did, which was to fall over into the water despite my fears and then to forget about my fears.

Dive into It

My camp counselor demonstrated many of the qualities and approaches you will learn about in this part of the book. As you begin to apply them in your family, your children will feel welcome support as they let go of their perfectionism. For yourself, remember to draw on the support of your partner and others around you—and on your own courage. Then lean over the edge of the dock and let yourself go.

What is more mortifying than to feel that you have missed the plum
for want of courage to shake the tree?
—Logan Pearsall Smith

Chapter 4

Encouragement Communicates Acceptance

Freeing your family from perfectionism involves creating an environment where everyone in the family feels acceptable. One way to do this is to show your children that you love them despite their mistakes.

Take Family Members into Consideration

Keep this basic psychological principle in mind as you travel the road to freedom from perfectionism: If it appears that you're taking a person into consideration, then he'll get the sense that he's important to you and will feel that you have a connection. As a result, his feelings of acceptance will rise, his self-esteem will improve, and thus he'll be more prepared to risk making changes and doing new things.

This principle explains why it's so important to listen to your child and understand things from his point of view. Another great way to let him know that you're taking him into consideration is for you to point out, relentlessly, anything and everything that you appreciate about him. Appreciative comments such as "I love how curious you are" or "I'm so glad you enjoyed playing with Rashid today" let him know that you value him. Because you're paying attention to what matters to him, he feels that he matters to you.

Offer Encouragement

In 1957, Rudolf Dreikurs said: Perfectionism is rampant today . . . and it is in this competitive drive to accomplish a moral and intellectual superiority that making a mistake becomes so dangerous. . . . If we can't make peace with ourselves as we are, we will never be able to make peace with ourselves. This requires the *courage to be imperfect* [italics added]. . . . *[1]

Dreikurs is the widely respected author of *Children: The Challenge.* What he is describing here is a process he called *encouragement:* literally, helping a child find the courage to do things differently by letting her know she is recognized and cherished. He wanted to teach parents how to help children feel acceptable as people, regardless of what their accomplishments might be. He realized that it's easier to try new things and risk making mistakes if you already know you're acceptable. This approach to childrearing is represented today in Don Dinkmeyer and Gary McKay's book, *Raising a Responsible Child.* For more information about this book, see page 46.

Psychology uses many words to describe the effects of encouragement. When encouraged, children feel *validated* as people, *affirmed* in being who they are, and *mirrored* and understood. In everyday language, they feel worthwhile, helpful, cherished, and loved. All of these come from recognizing children (and adults, for that matter) for who they are, rather than simply for what they can do or for whom we might want them to be.

One important point to remember: encouragement has to be based on something you honestly feel. The comment "It's nice to see you so excited about this project" can be either sickeningly sweet and hollow or uplifting, depending on what the person who says it is actually feeling.

The Difference Between Encouragement and Praise

Encouragement and praise are different. Encouragement is an expression of confidence in, and appreciation of, another person:

- "I know you can do it."
- "I really appreciate your help with these chores."
- "You're really fun to be with."

---

* Rudolf Dreikurs was part of a line of psychiatrists, psychologists, and parent educators that began with his mentor and colleague Alfred Adler almost a century ago. Adler was a younger contemporary and, briefly, a colleague of Sigmund Freud.

[1] Dreikurs, R. in Terner, J., & Pew, W.L. (1978). *The Courage to Be Imperfect: The Life and Work of Rudolf Dreikurs.* New York: Hawthorn Books, 289.

Statements that are encouraging frequently focus on our own feelings about the other person.

Praise, on the other hand, focuses mainly on our judgment of the other person's performance:

- "That's very good work."

- "I'll give you an A for how your room looks."

Avoid "Giving Grades"

If instead of giving a grade you say, "I really like how your room looks" (your opinion, not an absolute judgment) or "I really appreciate all the effort you put into this job," your child is more likely to feel recognized and good about himself for having done something worthwhile.

By cultural convention, schools use grades to assess a child's educational progress. Without arguing whether this is good or bad (we could argue about that for hours!), it's important to avoid grading in other areas of a perfectionist's life.

A young man whose perfectionism weighed heavily on his self-esteem was in tears one day in my office because his dentist had given him a C on one aspect of his home dental care. He was convinced that nothing would ever go well in his life.

Imagine the dentist saying instead, "I can see that you're paying some serious attention to taking care of your teeth; that's going to be a big help to you over the years. Here's something I'm concerned about, though, that I'd like you to add to the great effort you're making." How would the impact of this approach compare to the impact of a grade? (Maybe you could give this same kind of encouraging message to your child regarding dental care.)

There's nothing wrong with giving "gold stars" or incentives. Reward and punishment are commonly used to motivate people. But rewards and punishments have some built-in problems. Rewards often must be increased in order to keep children motivated. If a dollar motivates a child to clean his room today, next week it may have to be two dollars. If going to a movie works today, it may take buying a video game next week.

Working for rewards also tends to focus children too narrowly on outcomes and not enough on what they're actually contributing. For example, the point of putting a child in charge of dishwashing is not simply to get a job done but also to have the family run smoothly, so there will be time for everyone to have fun. In a reward system, though, the point becomes to get the reward.

Punishment, outside of the day-to-day limit setting parents need to do with any of their children, tends to create hostility, defensiveness, and power struggles, and so is typically a poor source of motivation, even though it may seem to work in the short run.

Perfecting their performance in order to please others is already a problem for perfectionists. This is why parents would be wise to move away from praise and toward encouragement. That's not to say you should never give praise. Praise won't hurt your child. It's just that the more *encouragement* you express, the more you help to build a base of self-acceptance in your child.

Make a Note of It

What do you say when you want to acknowledge something your child has done that you like? That you dislike? What does your partner say? Is there a reward system in place in your home? How is it working?

Do an experiment: Try using some of the encouragement language suggested in this chapter. It may feel artificial or forced at first, but try it anyway. What do you observe in your child after you've done this a few times?

Talk It Over

After you've made some of your observations, talk with family members about the encouragement process. Ask if they will agree to use encouragement language for a week, just to see what happens. Post encouragement language on notes around the house to help you remember alternative ways to communicate. It may feel like a joke at first, but talk it over after a week and ask if anyone felt a difference.

Encouragement Doesn't Mean Nagging or Hectoring

Like many terms in our culture, encouragement has come to mean more than one thing. Some people will describe their constant criticism and demands for improvement as encouragement for others to do better. I'm sure one of our country's founders, John Adams, had this in mind in his advice to his son John Quincy ("JQA"). David Greenberg writes that, in addition to enforcing a high-pressure education, the morally stern elder Adams also

" . . . *admonished his son to make 'a good account' of himself, and continued to hector him well into his adulthood. 'You come into life with advantages which will disgrace you if your success is mediocre,' Adams wrote to the 27-year-old JQA in 1794. 'If you do not rise to the head not only of your profession but of your country, it will be owing to your own Laziness, Slovenliness, and Obstinacy.'*

"[JQA's] copious diary entries reveal neurotically high ambitions and an obsessional level of self-reproach for not meeting them. 'Indolence, indolence, I fear, will be my ruin,' he wrote at age 20, voicing a refrain he repeated throughout his hard-working life." [2]

This is a good example of how *not* to encourage your child. It is likely that, if JQA had not had extraordinary intelligence, commitment, and energy, we would never have heard of him. The main effect of his father's hectoring was probably not JQA's outstanding success but rather his constant anxiety and self-reproach, and from Greenberg's description, his perfectionism.

Recognize Your Child's Good Feelings

Encouragement can come in many forms, not all of them verbal:

- a smile
- a wink
- a thumbs up
- a high five
- an arm around the shoulder
- a special card or note

All of these are ways of recognizing your child for his good feelings about something, and joining with him in those feelings. They

---

[2] Greenberg, D. "Daddy's Boys: JQA and W., the Presidents' Sons Running for President," *Slate,* 10 July 1999.

can also be signs of support and understanding when things have not gone well. They are gestures of connection that say, "I'm with you."

Show That You Cherish Your Child

When disciplining children, many parents abide by the principle "Separate the deed from the doer," meaning the behavior is not acceptable, but the child still deserves love. The encouragement process is the other side of this same coin. While it's certainly important to recognize your child's achievements, overcoming perfectionism begins with recognizing her as a cherished individual.

In this same vein, encouragement reflects progress and effort, rather than simply output. Commenting positively on the effort your first-grader has put into a handwriting exercise can help her to feel acceptable and good about herself, even if the letters are not perfectly formed. Doing this also sets the stage for improvement, since a child who feels good about herself will be more confident of her abilities to learn.

Many families have one child who does something well and another who does the same thing less well. This difference can occur for all kinds of reasons, although the basic fact is that all children differ in their capabilities. Comparing children to one another looks to some parents like a way of motivating a less capable child to do better, but the common outcome of these comparisons is discouragement. For a perfectionist, the message is clear: I'm not good enough as I am. The child may indeed try harder, but she will probably also intensify her perfectionism. A part of your encouragement process is recognizing each family member for who he or she is, separate from the others. Comparisons are rarely helpful. There is almost always someone in this world who can do something better than you, but that's always irrelevant.

Express Appreciation

Remember to thank your child for the efforts he makes, or for contributions to the functioning of the family. Of course, it's reasonable to expect your child to help with household chores. But rather than taking this participation for granted and not mentioning it, use the performance of a chore as an opportunity to say, "Thanks. It's really helpful when you do the dishes." You're giving a message of encouragement and acceptance.

> *You can never overdose on encouragement.*
> —W.L. "Bill" Pew

Celebrate Progress

Exalting in your child's successes, commiserating with her in defeat, saying what you appreciate about her, or simply telling her that you like her for who she is: these are all ways of encouraging her and therefore setting the stage for freedom from perfectionism. Through this process, your child will feel that she counts and is cared about.

Remember that a focus on progress, not results, helps in getting beyond perfectionism. Like the old gospel song says, "I ain't what I ought to be, but I'm better than I used to be, and I'm gettin' better every day."

 Read More About It

Punished by Rewards: The Trouble with Gold Stars, Incentive Plans, A's, Praise, and Other Bribes by Alfie Kohn (Boston: Houghton Mifflin, 1999). A controversial and thorough examination of the potential negative effects of rewards on children's self-esteem.

Raising a Responsible Child: How to Prepare Your Child for Today's Complex World by Don C. Dinkmeyer and Gary D. McKay (New York: Fireside, 1996). The latest edition of a highly readable and widely respected guide for parents; explains the encouragement process and a host of other ways to help children feel acceptable and competent.

Chapter 5

Letting Go of Power Struggles

Power struggles—the ongoing, recirculating arguments between parents and children (or between partners) that seem endless, pointless, and inescapable—are a staple in many families. This shouldn't be a cause for cynicism, however, since power struggles are avoidable in most cases and containable in others.

If your child is a perfectionist, you may find yourself in a power struggle with him for one of two reasons: 1) you often want your child to do certain things in certain ways, and he is resisting, or 2) your child is driving you crazy with his perfectionism and you want him to lighten up. In the first case, you may be contributing to your child's perfectionism; in the second, you may be reacting to it (which may also be contributing to it).

A Matter of Pride

Once they are underway, power struggles require the participation of both parties if they're to continue. You make a demand, your child resists, you resist her resistance—it's an endless cycle. Once the power struggle is underway, the topic of conversation usually gets lost. Instead of arguing about whether homework will get done ("this minute!"), you end up really arguing about who is in charge, or who will decide. This is why power struggles rarely resolve things, and why they so often leave us with hurt feelings and more determination to have it our way. Our pride gets wounded.

Perfectionist children want to please and be acceptable, yet they, like everyone else, have a sense of pride and independence. A dilemma that arises in many families is especially acute for a perfectionist child:

she feels she has to choose between pleasing her parents, thereby gaining their acceptance, and being her own person and making her own decisions, thereby risking disapproval for doing so. If, from her perfectionist standpoint, she has already decided that things must be done in a certain way, then her parents' insistence that she do something their way makes the dilemma all the more acute.

A Battle for Control

It might have been Rudolf Dreikurs who first said that in 99 out of a 100 power struggles between a parent and a child, the child will win. In the 100th case, the parent will wish the child had won. Children have more energy to devote to power struggles, so they are capable of wearing parents down. The battles quickly move from the problem at hand to the struggle over control, and the argument tends to keep coming up without ever being resolved.

Tamara was having problems in school because she was not handing in her homework. She had several assignments to do for her advanced placement courses and didn't think she had enough time to do each one perfectly. By not handing in her assignments, Tamara was delaying the inevitable judgment about the quality of her work.

Not wishing to displease her parents, Tamara had not told them about the homework problem. Of course, when her parents found out about it at a school conference, they were furious and confused about why she would be so defiant, and about how such a bright student could do such a "dumb" thing. Tamara was caught between her desire to have everything done the right way and her desire to have her parents' approval. She promised to do all of her work on time, but she continued to fall behind, and the result was an escalating battle with her parents. They did everything they could think of to reward her for getting her work done or to remove privileges if the work didn't get done. They were getting nowhere.

Tamara could see the value in getting her homework in on time. She was not lazy, and she was not typically hostile or defiant. Her concerns about the quality of her work may have been misguided, but they explained her reluctance to do her assignments, and her parents' pressure, in addition to being futile, made things worse.

In cases such as Tamara's, enlisting rewards and punishments in an attempt to get control and alter behavior is generally not effective. Too much is at stake. Psychologically, the problem is not that Tamara doesn't do her work but that she doesn't think her work will be good enough and therefore she won't be acceptable as a person. Pressuring her to do the homework without taking this into account amounts to pushing a very big rock up a very steep hill.

To oppose something is to maintain it.
—Ursula LeGuin

Drop the Rope

In the midst of a power struggle, it's hard to find any workable solutions. People can be much more creative and considerate of other viewpoints when they don't have to be defensive.

A tug-of-war will cease if you drop your end of the rope. Getting out of a power struggle means refusing to fight, and since you are the responsible adult, it falls on your shoulders to start the process.

Here's the kind of situation where you might drop the rope: Like most parents, you have probably tried to get your child to be a part of some activity that he wasn't interested in—playing the clarinet, perhaps, or playing baseball. You probably found yourself locked in an endless and fruitless battle. Realizing that the first step to solving this problem is getting out of the power struggle, try saying to your child: "Okay, I've decided not to fight with you about this any more. For now, you can decide what you'd like to do about this activity. Later, we'll talk about it again." Come back to it later, when things are going better. You're likely to get further with your point of view if you aren't in a fight. In the meantime, ask yourself why your child's participation is so important to you. You may have legitimate reasons for pushing for your child's participation, but consider this oft-repeated observation of social worker and family educator Miriam "Mim" Pew: "Anytime you want something for your child more than she wants it for herself, you probably won't get it."

Tamara's story, on page 48, is a good illustration of what can happen when parents take themselves out of a power struggle. Since rewards and punishments weren't working, they told Tamara that they were going to leave her homework to her, and that she could talk to her teachers about it if she chose. Meanwhile, they were going to see what they could do to have things go better around the house, including setting aside time to do things Tamara was interested in. They began to talk more openly about perfectionism and about each family member's feelings about doing well and making mistakes. They prepared themselves for the worst: that Tamara might do poorly in school or actually fail a class. As it turned out, the increasing warmth at home, plus a chance conversation between Tamara and her math teacher, who had had his own struggles with perfectionism, set the stage for Tamara to relax more, and for her talents to be more evident in school.

Talk It Over

Begin by talking with your child about a controversial situation. Pick a time when things are going relatively well, and begin by saying something like, "We seem to be arguing a lot about getting to hockey practice on time [or whatever the power struggle is about in your family]. I'm getting frustrated, and you must be, too. I'd like to talk about the situation and see if we can come up with a way to handle this that doesn't make us both crazy." If this is agreeable, and you're willing to hear whatever your child might say, you can ask what he thinks about the hockey program: Are there problems there? Does he like it? Does he think he's doing okay? What about being on time: does he think that's important? Is your child down on himself because he thinks he isn't good enough at hockey to please you, or the coach?

You and your child can also talk over some options that will keep you out of the battle if he continues to be late for practice. Should you set a limit on how late you're willing to leave for practice and simply not go after that time? (This is a very common, and frequently useful, way to establish a logically related consequence for his being late.) Or should you take him when he's ready and let him deal directly with his coach and teammates about being late? Discuss these options with him in a nonthreatening, matter-of-fact way and ask him for additional ideas. If the conversation doesn't lead to a decision, choose a solution and tell him you'd like to try it and see what happens.

Saying you want to get out of the power struggle doesn't mean that you intend to ignore your child or the problem that you've been fighting about. But your ongoing relationship with your child is more important than winning any particular point; when a battle has caused the relationship to deteriorate, it's time to give up the battle, repair the relationship, and then think of new possibilities for solving the problem.

Acknowledge Your Anger

Does all of this mean you shouldn't be angry with your child? No. Anger is a natural human emotion, and blocking it out would at best involve some form of psychological denial. We all get angry, and we all have different beliefs and rules about it, which we learned as part of our childhood emotional development:

- I deserve to be angry.
- I don't deserve to be angry.
- Good people don't get angry.
- Anger is a sign of evil.
- Getting angry means I'm losing it.

Perfectionists are sometimes afraid of anger, since they may believe that perfect people don't lose their temper. It's also easy to confuse the *feeling* of anger with angry *behavior.* Most of the rules people have about anger apply to angry behavior, which they may consider wrong, but the angry feelings themselves are just feelings. In addition, telling someone, in a respectful way, that you're angry is not the same as yelling at them or becoming violent.

It's okay for you to be angry, and it's also okay for your child to be angry. Anger is not a form of disrespect, it's just a feeling we have when things happen that annoy us or feel threatening to us. Certain behaviors, done in anger, can indeed be disrespectful—but then the behaviors are the problem, not the anger.

Whatever you may have learned about anger as you were growing up, it's a normal human response that helps you summon the energy you need to solve a problem. What's important is to acknowledge your anger and begin looking for solutions to the problem.

Expressing Your Anger

There are many ways to acknowledge and act on your anger without saying or doing hurtful things. Family communications experts often stress the use of I-messages for this. An I-message focuses on *the feelings you have* about something another person has done:

> "When I see you haven't made your bed yet, after you agreed to do it, I get really angry."

> "I worry about what will happen to your grades if you don't hand in your homework."

> "I don't like it when you play your music at full volume. I can't concentrate on what I'm reading."

The contrast to this would be a you-message, which is usually delivered in a demeaning tone of voice:

> "What's the *problem* here? Why haven't you made this bed yet?"

The word *you* may not actually appear:

> "How many times do I have to explain this?"

> "This place is a total mess."

Name-calling is a type of you-message:

> "What kind of an idiot would do this?"

Notice the accusatory finger-pointing in most you-messages: the focus is on the *person* rather than the *behavior*. In Chapter 4, I mentioned separating the deed from the doer. I-messages focus on what was done and how it affected you rather than on the doer. Using I-messages can help prevent defensiveness and arguing.

For many people, the problem in a relationship is not anger but its evil twin, contempt. Most research has shown that anger and disagreement can be very much a part of families in which everyone feels respected. What is most damaging to family ties is contempt—name-calling, scorn, icy silence, growing hatred. In our culture, contempt and anger are frequently intertwined. For many of us, when our parents were angry with us, we felt their contempt: we sensed that they did not like us, or that they saw some defect in us. These are the attitudes that breed perfectionism. Though it may be hard to imagine disentangling anger and contempt, it can be done. The use of I-messages helps, since it avoids accusatory name-calling.

Getting out of power struggles doesn't mean that you never get angry. It means recognizing that, when the power struggle is underway and the anger has become chronic, it's time to let go of your end of the rope.

I've learned . . . that being kind is more important than being right.
—ANDY ROONEY

What's the Anger About?

If the topic under discussion gets lost when a power struggle is underway, it's important to ask what the other person is angry about. Otherwise, you may end up endlessly arguing about arguing, or arguing about whether you have a right to be angry. If you practice the approaches described in this chapter, you'll be able to say something like, "I can see that you're really angry. Tell me what it's about and I'd be willing to talk it over."

This is important, because it's easy to misunderstand what someone's anger is about. My wife and I used to routinely find our arguments intensified by an exasperated sigh I made. It was some time before we discussed this, and when we did, she discovered that my sighs expressed my frustration with being unable to find the right words to say what I wanted to say. I discovered that what they had always meant to her, though, was that I thought she was stupid.

Make a Note of It

What do you say to others when you're angry about something? Do you act differently inside the family than outside it? Is your anger expressed as you-messages or I-messages? Jot down your observations over the next few days. Note whether your behavior starts an argument, keeps one going, or opens the way for respectful discussion.

Talk It Over

Ask other family members what they think about arguments the family gets into. Ask: Do the arguments resolve anything? How does everyone feel after an argument? Do you think we sometimes misunderstand each other's anger? Talk about I-messages and you-messages, and ask family members to come up with examples. Talk about ways family members can express concern about something or solve a problem without getting into fights. Agree to try using I-messages for a week or two, then check back with each other to see how it has gone.

Apologies

If I-messages express the impact someone has on you, an apology is a recognition of the impact you've had on someone else. It's like the encouragement process described in Chapter 4: you recognize a family member for who she is—a person with real feelings. Apologies can end a power struggle and launch a new attempt to solve a problem.

Some people view apologies as a form of giving in to the other person, or even as a way of giving them some power. But when they're expressed with genuine care and respect, apologies can defuse the *need* for power by disengaging yourself from pointless battles in order to pursue real solutions to problems.

A man should never be ashamed to say he has been in the wrong, which is but saying in other words that he is wiser today than he was yesterday.
—ALEXANDER POPE

Imagine, after you explode at your child over something she has done or failed to do yet another time, coming back at a calmer moment and saying, "I'm really sorry I lost my temper. I need to work on that, and I will. I was angry with you because I can't seem to get you to do this job, so instead of yelling at you about it, I'd like to see if there's a way to solve this problem. Do you have any ideas?"

Here, you acknowledge that what you did might have escalated a fight because it left both you and your child defensive. You don't excuse your behavior but look for solutions to what you were angry about. You change the focus from the fight to the problem at hand.

"Mistakes Were Made . . . "

You may be thinking, as you read this section, about the insincere apologies often made by public figures:

- "I've made some mistakes, but I'm ready to move on now and leave that behind."

- "I'm sorry if anyone was offended by my actions. I meant no harm."

There's no contrition in these apologies. In the first, the speaker seems to be ready to move on despite the pain he or she caused, and in the other, the offended person is apparently being told not to feel bad.

Genuine apologies are offered out of remorse and are attempts to connect with the other person at an emotional level. If you don't mean it, don't say it. If you have trouble feeling remorse because you're still upset about what the other person did, wait until you're feeling less defensive and can get a clearer perspective. You might want to talk over your hurt and angry feelings with your partner or an understanding friend in the meantime.

Take Time to Clear the Air

Remember, too, that sincere apologies may not immediately resolve the tension. Allow the other person to respond, and listen with understanding if she starts to tell you about her ruffled feelings. She may apologize in return, but don't expect or insist on that. The idea is to keep moving toward a solution to the original problem. If she does apologize, accept the apology gracefully and be careful not to use it to trigger you-messages that may only renew the battle. The goal is to clear the air about the angry exchange. That lays the groundwork for new solutions, and even a new level of a relationship.

Cooperation in Solving Problems

Getting out of power struggles clears the way for a cooperative effort at solving problems. Acknowledging your anger, apologizing for any contributions you've made to power struggles, and using I-messages all contribute to the environment of encouragement described in Chapter 4. They're ways of recognizing and accepting others for who they are while improving the chances that problems can be resolved.

Admitting you made a mistake has another major effect: it provides your perfectionist child with a model of the courage to accept that mistakes happen, that their results can be dealt with, and that you can still be a good person. Using I-messages and apologizing for mistakes also increases empathy. I-messages express your perspective to your child, and apologies express your understanding of your child's perspective.

A lot is happening as you begin to move beyond power struggles. First, you decide that your demands are being ignored, so instead of tugging on the proverbial rope, you begin to look for a different approach to the problem. Second, you step out of a power struggle with your child and clear the air for problem solving. Third, you model a course of action that is antiperfectionistic. It wasn't useful to express anger here, it didn't solve the problem, but the feeling of anger was a normal human response, so you apologize for expressing it in the particular way you did and you look for a new solution. This means you've taken your child's hurt and angry feelings seriously, and it means you've allowed yourself to be imperfect.

The ideal, of course, is to create an atmosphere in your home where problems are solved without anger. You may be able to do that over time—some families can, usually because they're using the kind of approaches described in this book, whether they learned them as adults or children. Meanwhile, the effort you make along these lines is much more significant than any slips that may occur along the way.

Make a Note of It

Look for an occasion to practice dropping your end of the rope in an ongoing power struggle. Try an apology, if one is needed and sincerely felt. What happens when you do this? Do things improve? Is it easier to resolve the problem? If so, give yourself a thumbs up. If not, keep at it—real change takes time.

You'll find more information on I-messages and family communication in *Raising a Responsible Child* and *The Dance of Anger: A Woman's Guide to Changing the Patterns of Intimate Relationships* (see pages 104 and 105). Although this second book is entitled "a woman's guide," it's a very readable resource for understanding and dealing respectfully with anger, whether you're male or female.

Chapter 6

Empathy Makes the Connection

Empathy is the act of seeing things from another person's perspective. You don't need to agree with the other perspective, and you don't need to give up your own perspective when you empathize. The capacity for empathy is a profound part of our humanity.

Empathy helps us to feel understood and connected to others, so it's a crucial piece of the plan for freeing your family from perfectionism. In addition, seeing something from another's point of view allows you to understand that person better.

> *You're right from your side. I'm right from mine.*
> —BOB DYLAN

Uncover Your Child's Motivation

Remember, whatever sense people make out of the world, they will act accordingly. If it seems to your child that he must do everything exactly right in order to be acceptable to you, then that's what he'll do. Of the many approaches to helping people change their behavior, the ones that work best are the ones that take into account what motivates the behavior in the first place. That's why learning to understand another person's perspective is so important.

You've probably already had some experiences where you've been able to see your child's world from his point of view. If he suddenly became reluctant to go to school in the morning, you may have discovered that a bully had begun taunting him there, that a teacher or classmate humiliated him, or that everyone was wearing certain clothes that he didn't own, and he felt out of sync (or out of style). The professionals sometimes call this school avoidance and the label is accurate as far as it goes, but it misses the point. To help your child regain the confidence to go to school in the morning, you have to start by finding out what makes it hard for him to go in the first place. Understanding things through your child's eyes doesn't mean excusing his behavior or letting it go. He still needs to go to school.

Understanding someone's behavior from his or her perspective is frequently confused with excusing the behavior. When we hear about a particularly brutal crime, we often ask, "How could anyone do that?" Answering the question by talking about addiction or depression or childhood abuse is not a way of excusing the behavior or letting it continue. Instead, it's a way of understanding more deeply what the problem is in hopes of preventing it in the future.

In the same way, when your child misbehaves, understanding the reasons behind that behavior *from your child's perspective* is the first step in devising a plan to prevent recurrences.

Nguyen was a straight-A student who put tremendous effort into getting all of his schoolwork done correctly, but he usually kept to himself at school. Nguyen's parents had begun to hear that Nguyen was getting friendly with gang members from his family's home country. Becoming alarmed at this, the parents tried in vain to set curfews and to ground Nguyen so he couldn't be with these boys.

One day, when Nguyen and his dad were playing cards together, his dad asked what the attraction of this gang was. Nguyen explained that he and other Asian kids at school were often harassed by other students, which made him angry, and the gang's ethnic pride and defiant attitude helped him feel stronger and able to retaliate.

Nguyen's perspective made sense to his dad, even though he objected to the gang and its behavior. His dad talked with Nguyen about his own experiences with discrimination, and his anger about it. They also were able to talk about ways to confront the issue and express pride in their ethnic background without doing things that were alienating and dangerous. The conversation was moving for both Nguyen and his dad. They agreed to talk some more, which they actually did over a period of time, even though in their culture families usually did little of this. Nguyen learned more about his dad and about their cultural heritage. Over time, Nguyen began pulling back from the gang, finally dropping it altogether.

Create an Emotional Bond

Empathy is more than understanding another person's perspective. When you communicate successfully that you are seeing things through the eyes of the person you're speaking with, an emotional bond is created.

Maybe you've had this experience: You come home at the end of a difficult day and your partner says, "You look really beat." Or you accidentally cut yourself and someone says, "Ouch!" These simple, direct emotional expressions can help you connect with the other person, and they can help you feel that someone is there with you in a difficult moment. Your experience is being mirrored by the other person, and that makes the experience seem more valid or acceptable. Naturally, you feel better.

The same is true for your child, whether she's had a particularly negative or a particularly positive experience. She, too, welcomes having her experience mirrored and accepted. When a dad spontaneously shouts "Awriiight!" in response to his son's excitement about his drawing, it's easy to imagine that his son feels cared about and supported.

Part of the power of empathy is in the sense of connection people experience when they feel understood. If someone understands us, that must mean we are understandable—that is, not crazy or out of touch, but normal. What a gift this can be.

To learn to empathize with your child, start by putting yourself in her shoes. What is it like to be her these days, or at this moment? Of course, you can't read her mind, so approach the subject with curiosity and a willingness to listen. "I wonder how you're feeling right now" or even "It seems like you're angry; am I right about that?" are valid questions and will usually work better than the provocative assertion "You're angry." You'll be coming to an understanding of the situation together, and this will help create a supportive bond. Remember, it's okay to be wrong when you guess how your child's feeling; making guesses starts a joint exploration that could eventually turn up something important.

Empathizing with your child is a way of being emotionally available to her. This will communicate increased acceptance of her as a person.

Learn What Your Child Is Feeling

Remember, you are trying to grasp what your *child* is feeling, not to figure out what you yourself would feel in his situation. You might, of course, feel the same way he does if you were in his shoes, and telling him this can help him feel your support. Still, what is important is how your child feels, whether you'd feel that way or not.

You may find that your child has feelings that are uncomfortable for you. If you don't like conflict, for example, and your child is angry, this may make you anxious. It may be helpful to remember that these are just feelings being expressed, and knowing about them is an important part of helping your child.

Convey Acceptance

Empathy is related to encouragement: being emotionally available to your child signals acceptance of who she is at a deep level. You can express empathy in many ways, verbal and nonverbal, just as you can express encouragement. A pat on the back when something has gone well, a grimace when your child describes something painful, a sigh of relief when an ordeal is over—all are ways of signaling your attention to your child's feelings.

What if you discover your child has feelings that come from a misunderstanding? Should you simply accept these feelings and leave it at that? You can accept your child's feelings for what they are and still help her move beyond those feelings if necessary.

Deanna had been acting discouraged and withdrawn for several days. Standing in the kitchen with her, her dad said, "DeeDee, you seem sad or something. Is everything okay, or is something wrong?" In the conversation that followed, her dad learned that Deanna had, for the first time since she'd been in school, started a math course that she found hard. When he asked, "What do you think about that?" he learned that Deanna had concluded that she wasn't as bright as she'd thought. Her self-image had begun to suffer as a result.

"Wow," said her dad, "I'll bet that was a real blow!" Then, after they'd thought this over together for a while, he said, "But you know, there is a different way to look at this that may help you feel better. You might have finally gotten to the place where math is challenging for you—which maybe it

should *be to stay interesting!" Seeing it this way made Deanna's struggles with math seem totally different to her, and she felt much better.*

Part of what allowed Deanna to feel encouraged was her father's acceptance of her initial feelings as understandable. He saw them from her perspective, even though he went on to talk about another perspective. Without this empathic support, things could have gone differently, even if her father had wanted to be helpful. He might have said to her, "Don't be silly, of course you're smart," thus ridiculing her thoughts. Even without ridicule, he could have negated her feelings by saying, "Well, don't let it get you down—just keep working at the math." He might have been correct that Deanna should keep working on her math, but the situation had already gotten her down, and it was hard for her to go on because she didn't think she was capable of doing it. Her father would have been responding to the problem at hand, but not to the *person* having the problem. In working with your child, it helps to keep this distinction in mind.

Make a Note of It

In conversations with your child or partner, teach yourself to listen with the third ear: in addition to the topic of conversation, make a mental note of the feelings being expressed—the *emotional content* of what's being said. If the feelings are hard to identify, ask the other person about them.

Ask yourself what these feelings say about your child or partner. Are they part of a pattern of feelings that occur frequently? Would you have the same feelings if you were in his shoes? Does this make his particular feelings right or wrong?

Make a note of how you feel about your child or partner's feelings. Do you get angry or scared, for example? If so, ask yourself what might have you feeling that way. You might also want to find ways to express these feelings to the other person. Use I-messages, so you both can learn more about each other's reactions.

Talk It Over

Discuss with family members your attempt to tune into the emotional content of family conversations. Ask them to work on this with you, and to be patient with you as you learn how.

Remember that learning empathy takes time, and it may feel arti-ficial at first. If one attempt doesn't feel comfortable, experiment with another approach the next time. Watch for your successes, even small ones. If by listening to your child with your third ear, you're able to identify a feeling that you normally would not have noticed, take heart. You've taken another step toward freeing your family from perfectionism!

> *The moment of change is the only poem.*
> —ADRIENNE RICH

Chapter 7

Looking Inward

In Part 1 of this book, you began to think and talk about the idea that you've had a significant influence on your child's development. In this chapter, you'll be invited to look more closely at what you expect of your child and how that might contribute to her perfectionism. You'll also explore how the hopes and fears that you and your partner have affect your relationship with each other and with your child, again perhaps contributing to a perfectionist environment.

Looking inward to explore these issues can be difficult, because it's very personal, so remember that your courage in doing this will allow you to develop greater capacities to help your child, and yourself.

Looking inward isn't done in order to be self-critical. It isn't a way of asking, "What have you done to your child?" Rather, it's a way to examine your ongoing influence on your child and to help you change it in useful ways.

Remember, you're reading this book because you're looking for ways to be helpful. That far outweighs any mistakes you may have made as a parent. If you feel sadness, or fear, about what your role has been, that's because you have a conscience—otherwise, you wouldn't care. And that's a good thing. Give yourself some respect and appreciation as you take an honest look inward.

This kind of self-examination is often easier and more effective if it's done in the company of someone you trust and with whom you feel reasonably comfortable sharing insights about yourself. If your partner has been participating with you in the discussions suggested in earlier chapters, a joint exploration of the issues in this chapter should come naturally, although not necessarily easily. If you do this together, make an agreement that you won't argue about what you find. Agree to simply listen and do some thinking after you talk. Agree that, if either of you feels accused or recognizes that you're becoming defensive, you'll stop for a day or two and then return to the conversation.

Whether you do this inward exploration alone or with someone else, here's an example of the kinds of things you'll be asked to consider in this chapter: Think about whether you ever make adamant statements such as the ones below, and allow yourself to consider what your child or partner may be feeling when you do:

- "I'd go right back and tell that person what I think."

- "When something hasn't gone well, you should just pick yourself up and get back to work."

- "Just sit yourself down and do it."

- "It doesn't have to be perfect, you know."

- "Get over it!"

- "I don't understand what your problem is. This is fine."

It isn't that these statements are wrong or irrational. The question is, what does your child hear? Is it something like, "I'm not strong enough" or "I can't do it right" or "I have the wrong ideas"? If so, you may be influencing her in ways you didn't intend. Can you think of similar opinions that you state often and strongly in your home? As you look honestly at the ways you interact with your child and other family members, you can begin to find areas where changes in what you say or do—sometimes simple changes—might help reduce their need to be perfect.

There is no excellent beauty
that hath not some strangeness in the proportion.
—FRANCIS BACON

Hopes and Fears

Everyone enters into relationships—whether with children, partners, or friends—with a set of hopes and a set of fears. You hope you'll receive nurturing and recognition from a friend or partner. Depending on how things have gone for you up to that point in your life, you may also have fears or concerns about whether you'll get these things. When you have children, you experience some fear about the responsibilities you are taking on, but you also hope your children will look up to you and want to be like you in certain ways. You hope they'll listen to you and take you seriously. Whether they do these things can have a profound effect on your self-esteem. Your frustrated hopes can become a source of anger.

As any parent knows, children bring excitement, spontaneity, and a level of chaos into the family. If you're a perfectionist, chances are you're not always happy about this. When your children threaten your need for order or when they endanger your self-image as a competent parent, they may ignite your old fears about not being good enough. You may feel threatened, and you may then become angry or demanding. This sets the scene for a mutual influence interaction: you have a need to feel competent, so you want your child to act a certain way; meanwhile, your child concludes that, to be acceptable, he must perform in this certain way. His perfectionism blossoms.

It doesn't take a perfectionist parent to set the stage for a child's perfectionism.

Ray is a police officer. Partly for reasons of personal pride, he has decided that his son, Tony, should also go to the Police Academy and join the force. Ray would then feel that he had done a good job of parenting and that he had made a good accounting of himself with his family.

Tony has no interest in a police career. He is heavily involved in his guitar playing, which Ray sees as just a hobby, and as a very disreputable career choice. Ray frequently fights with Tony about the guitar playing. Tony tries hard to please his dad. He is a perfectionist about his guitar music, always hoping that his dad will finally see it as a good thing. At the same time, he can't bring himself to consider police work, so he feels he'll never be acceptable to his dad.

Ray is not a perfectionist himself. He does hope to be seen as a good person and a valued member of his family. He may fear losing face if he can't seem to raise a son who fits in with traditional family ways. This means his self-esteem depends partly on having a son behave a certain way, and when Tony resists there is much anger on both sides. Tony is trying hard to please his dad without giving up something he values. The chronic anger leaves Tony wondering if his dad likes him, and he responds by pushing himself to be all the more accomplished on the guitar.

Frustrated hopes can lead to other kinds of behavior that set the stage for your child's perfectionism:

- Your child's growing sense of independence leaves you feeling unrecognized or disrespected as an authority. You become constantly critical and demanding. Your child feels he can never be good enough.

- Your need for recognition or admiration leads you to put your energies into your work outside of the home. You pay off-and-on attention to your child, who tries to please you and get more of your attention by being perfect.

Make a Note of It

What are your hopes in your relationship with your partner? With your children? Jot them down. Do you hope to be recognized, understood, seen as special, affirmed, cherished, looked up to, or depended upon? Do you want to be respected for being right, or in control of things, or fair-minded, or understanding? None of these hopes are inappropriate, but think about whether any of them lead you to make continual demands on your partner or children, or to have especially high expectations. Do you become disappointed in them for not meeting your needs?

Once you identify your hopes, make a note about how you respond to your partner and children when those hopes seem especially important to you. For example: If you feel you have to be seen as being right, what do you do when your children disagree with you? If you want respect for having everything in place and orderly, what do you do when your children are spontaneous, or forgetful, or clumsy (normal behaviors in children everywhere)?

What about fears? Are you secure about having your hopes fulfilled or fearful that they won't be? Does it seem, for example, that you can never get the respect you deserve, or that people never listen to you, or that no one will support you when you feel bad? If you expect certain things from your children, are they related to these fears?

Talk It Over

Talk with your partner about the hopes and fears you each have in your relationship and in your parenting. Approach this as an exercise in brainstorming. Check with each other to find out if you can state your hopes and fears honestly, and simply have them heard; no decisions or actions are necessary right now.

If you aren't used to highly intimate conversations about sensitive emotional topics such as these, this can be scary. If you're willing to take the plunge to a new level of depth and honesty, however, you may discover, as many people have, how good you feel about yourself for having done it. Chances are you'll feel much closer to your partner. In fact, the only way to get closer to someone is to let your guard down. If that turns out to be safe because each of you listens respectfully and takes seriously what the other is saying, then you've set the stage for freeing yourselves from perfectionism. That's because you begin to realize that you don't have to be perfect to be acceptable. It's worth the effort.

Have this conversation in whatever way suits you best. Go somewhere you won't be distracted. You can talk back and forth, or you might prefer to let one person have the floor without interruption, then let the other have a turn. Perhaps you'd feel more comfortable writing things down in letter form, using what you each write as the basis for a conversation later. Another option is to sit back to back, so body language and facial expressions are less evident.

Agree to discuss the topic again after a few days. You might even make a plan to have regular talks—every week, for example—so you can count on a forum for your thoughts. There isn't a right way here. You may have some other ideas about what would be most suitable for you. Only you and your partner can decide that.

One important way to make this process helpful, and likely to continue, is to mention things you like and appreciate about your partner. Let her know in what ways she really comes through for you, realizing your hopes. Tell her if some of your fears have proved groundless.

If you don't have a partner, or your partner refuses to participate, you'll need to find support through other people—a close friend or relative, a counselor or a group—who will help you (and hopefully your partner) build this level of emotional support into your daily life.

Gerald and Grace were both perfectionists whose marriage was strained because of their perfectionism. They were both successful lawyers who had been straight-A students in school and who were highly valued by their employers. The problem was that Gerald spent hours getting every detail of his work exactly right, while Grace was very social, involved in everything, and seemed to do her work effortlessly. Over time, Gerald began to feel bad about himself as he watched Grace and wondered why he had to work so hard. Grace, meanwhile, felt that she must not be doing things well enough, because Gerald was working so much harder than she.

Gerald wanted respect for his hard work and Grace wanted respect for how easily she did things. Instead, Gerald heard complaints that he was always working, and Grace heard complaints that she wasn't serious enough about work. Their frustrated hopes for admiration and respect, and their growing self-doubts, led to anger and wreaked havoc in their marriage. Once they recognized how their hopes were frustrated, and how they were making each other's perfectionism worse by their seeming rejection of one another, their appreciation for each other's strengths began to grow and they got back in touch with the many things they enjoyed about each other.

Family Stress

If you're relatively satisfied with your life, and generally feel good about yourself, and if the same can be said about your partner, then things probably run pretty smoothly in your home. But no family is entirely without stress and strain. Normal occurrences such as moving to a new home; a developmental milestone in your child's life, such as going off to school for the first time; or a death in the family will cause disorientation and turmoil for a time, but this tends to get better in due course.

There may be more chronic stresses, however, that you don't handle well, either because they're ongoing or because no one really does anything about them. Extreme examples of this are drug and alcohol abuse, constant arguments and name-calling that may lead to divorce, a parent's untreated depression or mental illness, or the chronic physical or emotional absence of one or both parents. Problems such as these can underlie a child's perfectionism, and they're the kind of things that frequently require outside help to resolve. If any of these are a part of your family, Chapter 9 (pages 79–87) can assist you in finding the help you need.

Identifying areas of ongoing family stress is an important part of looking inward. Ask yourself how you might be contributing to a stressful situation in the family, either by something you are doing or by something you notice but haven't acted on.

Parental Disagreement

Another area for self-exploration is your relationship with your partner. Parents can set the stage for their children's perfectionism by how they interact with each other, separately from how they act with their children.

Asha's perfectionism was an attempt to please two parents who seemed to be working at cross-purposes. Her mom was very demanding and set high standards, which she expected Asha to meet. Whenever she argued with Asha, though, her dad would tell her mom to lighten up and get off Asha's back. Asha's mom felt undermined, and a fight between the two parents would result. Her dad felt pushed out, and he became fearful for his daughter.

Asha didn't want to take sides in the argument because she wanted to stay connected with both parents and she wanted the fighting to stop.

Many of these chronic parental arguments are based on the frustration of hopes. Asha's mother may wish to be recognized as a competent parent, or she may want to prove she can be right about things. Her attempts to get Asha to do things her way may bring out in Asha's father a need to be a good protector, or perhaps to fend off assaults on his own self-esteem. He jumps in to protect his daughter and ends up in a fight with his wife that Asha tries her best to stop.

We all live in a web of relationships and have hopes and fears about each one. It helps to learn something about these hopes and fears, because when there is a clash, what reduces one person's fears often increases the other's, and vice versa. Asha's mother might feel better if she could get Asha to do what she wanted her to do; to Asha, this would mean giving up her independence, and to her father it would mean allowing his daughter to be run over. All three of them have their pride at stake. Seeing the different perspectives allows them all to find ways to meet each other's needs without giving up on their own. It also sets the stage for reducing the ongoing anger and resentment.

Make a Note of It

In the last "Talk It Over" on pages 66–67, you identified the hopes that you and your partner each have. Now take some time—several days or more, if you need them—to think about how your various hopes relate to each other. Can you see how they might be at cross-purposes at times and lead to conflict between the two of you? When this happens, what effect do you think it has on your child? On your relationship with your child? On your relationship with your partner?

Try this: The next time you find yourself feeling angry with your child or partner, check in with yourself to see what other feelings you might have. Are you feeling personally offended? Sad? Scared? Cornered? Alone? What hopes of yours are being thwarted? What fears do you have?

Don't worry if this exercise is difficult or confusing at first. The effort you are making to search for answers is a sign of your family's importance to you. Stick with it, and remember that talking it over may give you new insights.

Talk It Over

Since my wife and I are both psychotherapists, it would be easy for us to get into the habit of psychologizing each other during arguments—that is, analyzing the reasons for each other's behavior and generously offering our brilliant insights. Of course, the underlying message would be, "You see, this really isn't *my* problem, it's yours!" For years, we have followed a rule against doing this.

As you talk over the emotional underpinnings of family relationships discussed in this chapter, consider setting your own ground rules. You may want to adopt our rule of "no psychologizing," for instance, since telling your partner that you know why she does something typically comes off as arrogant and seems to put all the blame on her. Steer clear of statements that begin with "You always . . . " or "You never . . . " or the almost irresistible "You're just like your mother." These statements refer more to your partner's character rather than to the behavior you're concerned about. They might feel threatening to your partner and won't lead to a cooperative and respectful exchange.

Share what you've jotted down about yourself in the previous "Make a Note of It" exercise. If your partner has also done the activity, listen to her list with interest, and without judgment. What's it like for you to hear what your partner has to say? Is it surprising? Sad? Scary? Talk about this, being careful to avoid implying that your partner should not have these feelings, or that they're wrong in some way.

This mutual exploration, if done with an attitude of cooperation and learning, can give you helpful information, and it can tremendously improve empathy.

If you're comfortable talking with your partner about some of these emotional insights, you can bring them up with your child as well:

- "Sorry I yelled at you about spilling your water. I think I get really scared about things getting messy, about not being able to keep everything in order. I realize that's my problem. Thanks for cleaning it up!"

- "Here, why don't you try doing this while I watch? I guess I get nervous about how it's going to turn out, so I'm always wanting to do it myself!"

These messages, which are based on what you've learned from looking inward, allow your child to see that we all have our imperfections, that these can be dealt with, and that you're still acceptable as a person. If that's the message you're sending, you're on the road to freedom from perfectionism.

Chapter 8

Beyond a Perfectionist Culture

When you see an awards ceremony for the Olympic Games on TV, what story evolves as you listen to the commentators describe the event winners as they take the stand for their medals? Are there three elated athletes, who've come within hundredths of a second of each other, recognized as the best in the world? Or is there one gold medallist, plus two athletes who came so close but must make their peace with losing?

The Winner-Take-All Attitude

One young perfectionist in my office exclaimed, through tears of anger and frustration, "You don't see stories on the sports pages about football players who played a good game. The stories are about being a winner. If you didn't win, the story is about being a loser, or there's no story at all."

As a parent, you can set the stage for perfectionism in your child, but you're getting plenty of assistance from society. In what has become a culture of celebrity, where people look for their 15 minutes of fame, there is intense pressure to be on top. The adulation and financial rewards that winners gain are the perfectionist's worst nightmare: you are either perfect or you are worthless.

- Parents hire coaches and private tutors, not just because their child may need remedial help, but because the parents want the child to have an *edge* in life.

- A school counselor laments that the message to children has gone from "Be the best you can be" to "Be the best."

- At the ballfield, parents scream at their children, or do worse things, when a play isn't to their liking.

Family stress is only intensified by the constant societal pressure to be the best. Children are not only under the gun to be outstanding, they are frequently overscheduled and rushed in the limitless drive for success.

In some places, parents who recognize the destructive aspects of all this pressure have joined together to try to change things, at least in their community. Family therapist and author William Doherty has helped members of one suburban community to create a Family Life First group, whose aim is to support reasonable limits on extra-curricular activities and give family connections some attention.

Despite pressures to the contrary almost everywhere you turn, there are things you can do to lessen the cultural influences on your family, and they needn't involve removing yourself from society. Here are some suggestions to get you started.

Make a Note of It

Begin thinking about your own and your partner's attitudes about winning and being the best. Jot down examples of these attitudes. Also jot down any examples outside the family that may be influencing you.

Is your family overscheduled? Make a list of all the things, including school and work, that your family does. If you are a visual person, block out the time you spend on these activities on a weekly calendar page, using different colors for different family members. Are there any blank spaces left? Do you or your children have any goofing off time? How do you view this: as relaxation or as idleness in a negative sense?

Talk It Over

Ask your children what they think of the winner-take-all attitude in society. Do they see it? Does it seem reasonable and natural? Discuss examples from your notes, both outside and within your family.

Ask your children whether they feel overscheduled. Who wants a particular activity more—your children or you? What do they think you would say if they dropped out of an activity? What *would* you say? Would they even consider dropping out? Why not?

Discussions such as these serve two purposes: they help everyone recognize that a problem exists, and they set the stage for more conversations about how to make changes that might be helpful. Becoming more conscious of outside pressures gives your children the perspective of observers. This helps them realize that the pressures may be common but that they're not simply a part of the natural universe. Family decisions to approach things differently help empower everyone to make changes. You may run into complications in dealing with the problem of overly busy lives, so have a discussion with your partner before including the rest of the family. First, you'll need to decide whether it's important to you or your partner to have your children highly involved in activities. If so, does this have to do with your own perfectionism? Or are you concerned that your child may have a talent that you'll fail to encourage? Are you going along with pressure from your children about being involved in various activities because you don't want to upset them by setting limits?

If you're concerned about your children's level of involvement, then these issues need to be worked out so that you can come up with a plan. Make sure to work on your own perfectionism, following the guidelines in this book. Recognize that if your child has an obvious talent for something and an interest in it, and the resources are available to develop the talent, you may decide to help him focus on that interest by limiting other activities. Finally, even if your child has multiple talents and interests, you may need to set limits on his involvement, for several reasons:

- In a world where choices are seemingly endless, no one can do everything, and learning to set limits is an important part of a child's development. This may involve increasing your own ability to make choices in your life so that you can model this for your child.

- If your child is a perfectionist, limiting his involvement may help him to grapple with the idea of letting go and learning that he can survive not being good at everything. More importantly, you will be helping him to remove himself from some of the outside pressures to be perfect.

- Simplifying your lives is a way to greater tranquility and may allow your child to experience more enjoyment for something he really likes, without the need to run from one activity to another.

If your child, rather than you or your partner, is the primary person pressing the overinvolvement, discuss why this might be. Are there social pressures? Your child may say, "Everyone is doing this," or "I can't be popular if I don't do this," or "I'll be out of it if I don't participate." Is that a show of perfectionism—having to be the best at everything? You will need to investigate this in conversations with your child so you'll know how to approach the problem. Remember, the reasons for your child's overinvolvement may be entirely legitimate and should be acknowledged as such, but we still have only 24 hours in the day. You may ultimately need to set limits on outside involvements. Talk about cutting back to see what will happen. Agree to try it out for a period of time and to check in regularly to see how everyone is taking the changes.

Initially, there may be some anger and resentment about the limits, and your perfectionist child may have some fears about what will happen. Acknowledge this and accept it as you explore the changes you've decided on.

We all want our children to have the best opportunities, and to get the most out of life. The dilemma, living as we do in a competitive culture with seemingly unlimited resources, is in the potential to do so many things that we *overdo*. We then end up destroying the harmony and tranquility in our lives, and ultimately even risk our health. Modeling limit-setting and choice-making for our children is both healthy and necessary. At the same time, there is no easy resolution to this dilemma, and working it out in your family may take time.

The limits you want to set are not meant as punishments. No one has done anything wrong by being overinvolved. You are considering these questions because overinvolvement threatens family connections and can be a reflection of unhealthy perfectionist strivings. Be sensitive to the fact that some of your child's activities involve commitments to teammates or group members, and that withdrawing from these may hurt the group. If the changes are going to involve these activities, they may need to be put off until a natural breaking point comes.

Where Does the Pressure Come From?

The winner-take-all attitude has many roots in our society. It's the kind of attitude that takes on a life of its own. By now, the idea that you're either in the race to win or you're an outsider seems almost a part of the natural order of things. Undoubtedly, part of the problem comes from the increasing tendency of our market economy to turn people into commodities—a target market, something to be bought and sold. If you're selling something, you want more people to buy it. This means it's profitable to make people want to buy what you're selling, and one way to do this is to make your product seem like the key to success and acceptance in life. You want people to think they'll be admired if they wear the right clothes, have the right equipment, take the right vacations, drive the right cars, see the right movies, and on and on.

Psychologist and author David Walsh has been concerned for years about the influence of the media on family life. In his book *Selling Out America's Children,* he argues that the increasing amount of violence and sex on television, and the increasing focus on the drama of winners and losers, reflect the increasing amount of attention-getting content needed to keep viewers available for advertisers. The more nurturing, affirming, and connection-building aspects of human life are eliminated in favor of the self-gratifying I'll-get-mine impulses popularized by the media.

There's a paradox in this cultural tide that hits perfectionists especially hard. Pushing yourself to the top means pushing everyone else down, and it's lonely at the top; competitors are not likely to offer opportunities for the feelings of acceptance that perfectionists are struggling for in the first place. Our culture takes pride in individualism—being your own person and speaking up for your needs—but often turns community-building and personal connections into spare-time pursuits that get ridiculed for being "soft." The capacity for empathy is seen as an obstacle to the self-enhancement that our culture promotes as necessary for winning.

Talk It Over

Discuss with your partner and your children the pressures you may each be feeling to have certain things in life, including the pressures created by advertising. How is this pressure affecting your family life and the life of each family member?

Classroom teachers sometimes explore these issues with students; ask if your children have had such discussions in school. If so, ask them what they learned. What conclusions have they come to?

Discuss everyone's ideas and opinions. What could be changed about your family's buying habits, and why? What do your children think about not wearing the latest fashion or having the latest gadget?

Marcie and Josiah decided that, with the family's limited income, their children's demands for things they saw on TV had become too great. They sat down with everyone and made a plan: They would watch only 10 hours of TV a week (an arbitrary number that suited the family's schedule), distributed any way the children wanted, to be decided in advance when the Sunday newspaper's TV guide came out. The family had only one TV, so the children would take turns each week making the viewing decisions. Marcie and Josiah would talk over the decisions, but only restricted the more violent and sexually explicit programs. They also decided to watch some of the shows with the kids and talk over the program content, the advertisements, and whatever products were being showcased by the program itself.

Over time, Marcie and Josiah felt they were playing more of a guiding role in their children's lives, and they got to know more about their children's world. The children were not especially happy about the system, but they could generally keep up with the popular shows. The older daughter began taking an interest in the sales pressures in these programs, and she was a star in class when the teacher did a unit on media literacy. The children began to see in a different light the pressures from the media and from schoolmates to have the latest games or toys, and they felt better about not having more of these things.

Balancing Family and Culture

No one can escape the influences of culture. As your children grow up and move out into the world, they are inevitably influenced by others, and by what they see and hear around them. Still, their ability to recognize and make choices about these outside pressures is greatly affected by family attitudes and experiences. You can help them become informed observers, and even informed consumers. Other than the endless stream of money it requires to keep up, there is nothing inherently wrong with wearing the latest fashions, for example. For perfectionists, the problem is feeling that one *must* have the correct things in order to be acceptable. Although cultural influences are profound, the process of freeing your family from perfectionism will ultimately help free them from the negative pressures of the culture as well.

 ## Read More About It

Take Back Your Kids: Confident Parenting in Turbulent Times by William J. Doherty (Notre Dame, IN: Sorin Books, 2000). Doherty discusses some of the societal pressures that can make parents feel they're losing control of child rearing, and suggests ways parents can regain a sense of family harmony in the face of social pressures for overinvolvement.

Fighting Invisible Tigers by Earl Hipp (Minneapolis: Free Spirit Publishing, 1995). This guide for teens on coping with and preventing stress is useful for parents, too.

Selling Out America's Children: How America Puts Profits Before Values—and What Parents Can Do by David Walsh (Minneapolis: Fairview Press, 1995). This book explores the profound influence of profit-driven media on the development of values and offers some tips for parents on introducing and maintaining values that are important to the well-being of their children.

Chapter 9

When Professional Help Is Needed

Some perfectionists, though not a majority, suffer from mental and emotional disorders. In this chapter, you'll learn how to find out if these other disorders are present and how to find help if they are. This brief overview is offered to help you decide if assistance beyond the scope of this book would be useful. This chapter is different from others in the book; there are no activities for you to do, but you'll find information and resources that may be useful.

Is Perfectionism a Mental Disorder?

In a word, no. *Perfectionism* is a term that describes a certain group of personality characteristics. Although perfectionists are not typical (meaning the majority of people are not perfectionists), they are not abnormal in the sense psychologists mean when they describe something as pathological. Perfectionism is an unhealthy, burdensome set of behaviors, thoughts, and feelings, but it isn't a disease.

As mentioned earlier, perfectionism can range from mild to severe. If your child exhibits extreme perfectionism, any psychological condition she has may be more pronounced because of her perfectionism, or the psychological condition could be making the perfectionism worse (or both). If your child is a perfectionist and also has a mental disorder, both the mental disorder and the perfectionism can be significantly diminished with professional help. The same is true for you if you're experiencing both of these.

Of course, it's best not to *assume* that any extreme behavior you observe is necessarily a sign of either perfectionism or a mental disorder. It might or might not be. People may do the same things for different reasons. Constantly arranging things in exact locations on one's desk, for example, may be a sign of perfectionism, but it could also reflect obsessive-compulsive disorder, or depression, or avoidance of a threatening assignment, or even simple boredom. Sometimes professional testing, called an assessment, may be needed to tell the difference.

Parallel but Separate Tracks

Although research scientists sometimes mention perfectionism when they talk about a broad range of mental disorders, there is no necessary relationship. This means that these disorders can also be seen in people who aren't perfectionists and that many perfectionists have none of these disorders. The following pages review some common mental disorders and suggest how perfectionism might relate to them. These disorders run on parallel tracks with perfectionism; when a perfectionist has the disorder, they interact but they remain separate.

Obsessive-Compulsive Disorder

Obsessive-compulsive disorder (OCD) is listed first here because it frequently includes behaviors that could be described as perfectionist. OCD is a kind of anxiety disorder that includes compulsively and ritualistically performed behaviors and/or obsessive, intrusive thoughts. People with OCD may, for example, recheck their work many times or wash their hands over and over. The necessity to be perfect can make these OCD symptoms worse, and OCD can drive perfectionist behaviors and thoughts to a dysfunctional intensity.

Anxiety and Panic Disorders

People with anxiety disorders and panic disorders feel highly anxious and scared even when no obvious threat is present. OCD is one of these disorders, but there are others, and their symptoms vary. People who have anxiety or panic attacks, for example, experience intense, periodic episodes of rapid heartbeat, shortness of breath, lightheadedness, terror, and other symptoms. Anxiety may also appear as a nervous stomach, headaches, a flushed face, or in other forms. The need to be perfect can greatly intensify these anxiety feelings, and anxiety disorders can overload an already stressed perfectionist.

Depression

Depression is a mood disorder. Its opposite is not necessarily happiness but a general sense of vitality or aliveness. The heavy burdens of perfectionism, with its constant vigilance against failure, can rob someone of vitality and can intensify depressed feelings. The hopeless feelings that go with depression can heighten a perfectionist's sense of discouragement. Research has shown that certain types of perfectionism are associated with higher rates of suicide. It is depression, though, and not simply the hopelessness of never being perfect, that leads someone to this extreme.

Addiction

Addictions to various chemicals or behaviors, such as sex or gambling, can be a relentless pursuit of a perfect escape. For some people, addictions soothe emotional pain; for others, addictions provide a feeling of aliveness in an otherwise emotionally deadened life. Perfectionism can intensify the compulsive qualities of addictions, and addictions can soothe the pain of not being good enough or provide an escape from the numbing necessity to constantly pursue perfection.

Eating Disorders

Eating disorders are attempts to control something very basic about oneself, the need to eat, sometimes with the idea of gaining the perfect body shape. People with eating disorders may compulsively overeat, undereat (anorexia), or overeat and then induce vomiting (bulimia). Research has shown perfectionism to be common among people with eating disorders. In a particularly vicious cycle, a perfectionist's fear of being unacceptable can be made acute by the alarm an eating disorder causes in others, and yet the pursuit of perfection drives a person to lose just a bit more weight.

Body Dysmorphic Disorder

An obsession with one's appearance, whether related to weight, body shape, or some difference from the norm, is sometimes diagnosed as Body Dysmorphic Disorder. Any difference is seen as a defect to be gotten rid of by exercise, dieting, surgery, or other means. This condition may be on the rise, and it's made worse by cultural influences.

Perfectionism can also make this condition worse, since having a flawless body can be seen as the route to full acceptance, and since the intense sensitivity to small differences can make a perfectionist more aware of flaws that need to be overcome.

Other Disorders

Perfectionism is sometimes an outcome of childhood trauma—an attempt to be so good that violence will stop, or an attempt to preoccupy oneself in the face of trauma. For this reason, perfectionism and post-traumatic stress disorder (PTSD) can sometimes go together. Perfectionism has also been shown to play a role, for some people, in relationship problems, sexual dysfunctions, migraine headaches, and workaholism. Again, many perfectionists have none of these problems, and many people with such problems are not perfectionists.

Telling the Difference

The list of disorders you have just read is not meant to be exhaustive, and many more psychological factors are involved than those listed here, most of these having little to do with perfectionism. How, then, can you tell if a mental disorder is present?

Mental and emotional disturbances may come and go in some people, but when they're present they tend to be all-consuming. If your child seems totally preoccupied by his perfectionism, or if it frequently gets in the way of his happiness or his ability to enjoy life, this would be a reason to see that he gets a psychological assessment for mental disorders. If there is a family history of mental disorders of any kind and you're concerned about your child's behavior, this also calls for an assessment. The same is true if you notice any vegetative signs—the medical term for changes in such things as his patterns of sleep or eating, his bowel or sexual habits, his levels of energy, or his interest in things, including both increases and decreases in any of these. Psychological testing can help you determine if there are serious disorders present that can and should be treated.

Testing

The first step in getting psychological help is to find out what the problem is so you can consider options for treatment. This is done in a face-to-face interview with a mental health professional or by taking a paper-and-pencil test, or both. These interviews and tests vary in cost. Check to see whether they're covered by your insurance. They should be done by licensed professionals who are skilled in diagnosis. Psychologists have the most extensive formal training in diagnostic procedures. On pages 85–86, you'll find guidelines for locating professionals who do testing and treatment. Again, check your insurance to see what professional services they cover.

Treatment

If you have found that a mental disorder is present, there are several options for treatment. In many cases, the person who does an assessment can also do therapy or recommend someone who can. Psychologists, psychiatrists, social workers, marriage and family therapists, counselors, nurse-practitioners, and pastoral counselors may be trained to do psychotherapy and family therapy. If medications are needed for conditions like depression or anxiety disorders, or if hospitalization is necessary for conditions like advanced eating disorders, the services of a medically trained psychiatrist will be required. Licenses, degrees, and levels of training can vary greatly. The best way to find a professional to help you or your child is to ask trusted friends or family members if they know of someone they'd recommend. (See other recommendations for finding a mental health professional on pages 85–86.)

Going for professional help can be difficult. We're all a little embarrassed to say that we or our children need help with emotional issues. Fortunately, attitudes about this kind of treatment, which can bring enormous relief and healing into people's lives, are changing for the better as more people make their experiences public.

How do you know if a professional is good? You should consider the person's education, experience in working with the problems you're concerned about, and licensure by a board that is responsible for maintaining training standards and investigating ethical violations. Beyond these basic qualifications, here are some things to keep in mind:

- Don't hesitate to consult with a professional to see if you like him or her before going ahead with therapy. Depending on the professional and the issues involved, you may be able to do this in a phone conversation or during an initial appointment. Ask any questions you have about procedures and costs.

- Your health insurance may cover some or all of the costs of these visits. Check with your insurance agent or company benefits administrator about outpatient mental health coverage, and see if the coverage applies wherever you go or only within the group of professionals who are part of your plan.

- Testing situations can feel impersonal. Make sure the professional answers your questions and is sensitive to your needs.

- When it comes to treatment, there should be good chemistry between you and the therapist. Specifically, you should feel listened to and feel that your concerns are respected. You should not feel that you're being given a one-size-fits-all approach. If the chemistry is not there, keep looking.

- If the appointments will be for your child, find out how you will be a part of the process. You've brought your child in because you're concerned about her well-being, so except for the details of any particular session, you should be informed about your child's progress. This may be done in a separate session with you (or you and your partner), or by including you in one of your child's sessions. Remember, however, that individual sessions are covered by privacy rules, meaning that except for certain court orders or when a client threatens violence against someone, the therapist is legally and ethically required to keep the sessions confidential. This rule exists so people can feel free to talk about anything they want. However, in most states, if a minor reports abuse, the professional must communicate this to law enforcement officials or a county social service agency.

- It's not always easy to tell whether progress is being made in therapy. The process can be painful, because of the emotional topics that come up, and it may take some time before the client feels better. The goals of therapy vary, depending on the problem, so you may want to ask about this. Don't hesitate to ask about your child's progress and talk with the therapist about your concerns.

- If you don't feel listened to and respected, or if you feel your questions about yourself or your child are not being answered to your satisfaction, find another professional to work with. There is no excuse for lack of respect, and your problems are important and deserve appropriate attention.

Resources for Finding a Mental Health Professional

If no friend or family member can suggest a good mental health professional, here are other ways you can find one:

- Ask your doctor or another health care professional for references.

- Ask your child's teacher or school counselor. They can draw on experience from their consultations with mental health professionals about students.

- Ask a clergy person from your religious faith.

- Ask people in any support group you belong to, such as a parenting group, Alcoholics Anonymous, or Al-Anon.

You can also check out the information sources in your community:

- Call the office of the state association for psychologists, marriage and family therapists, or social workers. They frequently have referral lists.

- Call First Call for Help, a comprehensive resource service for people wanting to know where to get help with personal needs. Most large communities in the United States have this service, and it's listed in the phone book.

- You can also consult the Yellow Pages under psychologists, physicians/psychiatrists, marriage and family therapists, social workers, or counselors.

National professional associations frequently have lists of local professionals, and some also have Web sites and literature about common disorders. Here are some national offices in the United States:

- **American Psychiatric Association**
  1400 K Street NW
  Washington, DC 20005
  1-888-357-7924
  www.psych.org/public_info/index.cfm

American Psychiatric Nurses Association
Colonial Place Three
2107 Wilson Boulevard, Suite 300-A
Arlington, VA 22201
(703) 243-2443
www.apna.org

American Psychological Association
750 First Street NE
Washington, DC 20002
1-800-374-2721
www.apa.org/psychnet

National Association of Social Workers
750 First Street NE, Suite 700
Washington, DC 20002
1-800-638-8799
www.naswdc.org

TherapistLocator.net
American Association for Marriage and Family Therapy
1133 15th Street NW, Suite 300
Washington, DC 20005
(202) 452-0109
www.aamft.org/TherapistLocator/index.htm

Information on the resources available from Canadian professional organizations can be found at the following Web sites:

Canadian Association of Social Workers: *www.casw-acts.ca*

Canadian Psychiatric Association: *www.cpa-apc.org*

Canadian Psychological Association: *www.cpa.ca*

Mental Disorders Are Not Failures

For perfectionists especially, it can feel like a personal failure to need the services of a mental health professional. But mental disorders are not character flaws, signs of moral failure, or failures of any sort at all. In some cases, they're caused by biological conditions of the brain. In all cases, they involve particular sets of interpretations of the world and of relationships. Seeking help does not make you or your child less of a person. To the contrary, your courage and resourcefulness in getting the help you need to solve problems are among the strongest of human virtues. If you or your child enters into psychotherapy for any of these disorders, you will have some hard work to do, and it may take time. This work, though, will not be much different from what you've done so far if you've done the activities suggested in this book. It will be personalized for your particular needs, and there will be someone to guide you on your way.

If the therapy you participate in is helpful, you'll find that both the perfectionism and any mental disorders will be significantly diminished. There can be a combination effect in this: reducing the perfectionism can take some of the emotional fuel away from a mental disorder, and reducing a mental disorder can make it easier to work on reducing the perfectionism.

If you have courage and are open to change, you can find the help you need. Keep looking.

Read More About It

Darkness Visible: A Memoir of Madness by William Styron (New York: Random House, 1990). A brilliant writer's intensely personal and informative account of his experience with depression.

An Unquiet Mind: A Memoir of Moods and Madness by Kay Redfield Jamison (New York: A. A. Knopf, 1995). A penetrating and an informative account by a respected psychiatrist of her own experience with manic depression.

When Nothing Matters Anymore by Bev Cobain (Minneapolis: Free Spirit Publishing, 1998). This resource for parents and teenagers explains what depression is and how to get help.

The Anna Westin Foundation
250 Prairie Center Drive
Eden Prairie, MN 55344
(952) 946-1131
www.annawestinfoundation.org
This organization is an excellent source of information, for both parents and young people, about eating disorders and what to do about them.

Chapter 10

Losses and Gains as You Let Perfectionism Go

Perfectionism, like any personality characteristic, is part of a person's sense of identity. If you're a perfectionist, you may not like the fact that you constantly sweat the details of whatever you're involved in, but that's who you are, and giving it up means changing your sense of yourself. You lose the identity you're used to. In doing so, you're likely to experience a period of uncertainty and adjustment: Can I get comfortable with a new identity? Or is the old one really what I want?

Freeing your family from perfectionism is a process of changing the way you *all* see yourselves—your *family identity*. Perfectionism is not a rational choice on anyone's part. It's something that develops as part of a person's struggle for acceptance. Once it has become a part of who you are, it's difficult to let go of. You can only cope with the change in identity and the loss of the functions that your perfectionism has performed in an environment in which you can feel acceptable regardless of your failings. Acknowledging these losses with other family members helps you see what is needed in order to feel safe about moving ahead.

What Might Be Lost?

Perfectionism can serve several functions, and the thought of losing any of them makes overcoming perfectionism a very difficult task:

- At its most basic level, perfectionism is what a person does to gain acceptance. No one would be willing to give that up without something to replace it.

▨ Many perfectionists keep themselves at an emotional distance from others by the constant stream of tasks that they believe have to be done right. Emotional distance keeps the person safe from judgments, and everyone wants to feel safe.

▨ A perfectionist can have an ongoing sense of identity as a person who doesn't make mistakes and who therefore deserves respect and acceptance. No one wants to risk a loss of identity.

▨ For some people, perfectionism functions as a constant resistance to the unpredictability that comes with an imperfect and changing world. We all need to have a sense of security, and the prospect of losing it can be frightening.

Freeing your family from perfectionism is a process in which you build an environment of acceptance: acceptance of one another as people, and acceptance of mistakes as a normal part of living. This environment of acceptance sets the stage for coping with the losses that come with giving up perfectionism. It means that people will feel lovable even if they aren't perfect, and they'll realize that they can be good at something even though they make mistakes. Reducing judgments and criticism and increasing encouragement all help people feel safer about emotional closeness. An accepting environment in which there is ongoing dialogue and interest in one another's lives reduces the sense of unpredictability and turmoil in the family and increases the sense of connection and empowerment to solve problems.

Jaime is a bright 11-year-old who has worked hard with his family to overcome his perfectionism. For years, he pressured himself to go over and over his work so it would be perfect. In class, he usually had the right answers to the teacher's questions, but on the few occasions when he didn't, he was depressed and miserable for days afterward. A family conversation about this problem revealed that Jaime had a reputation as the one with all the answers, and that was almost the only way he was recognized.

Jaime could only let go of his perfectionism after several discussions with his family about what might happen if he were no longer known as the smart kid in school. His mother reminded him that he had several interests, and that there might be others in the class who shared them. When Jaime began to accept the loss of his "smart-kid" identity, he also began to relax more. He found out he could be smart without needing to have a reputation for it, and he did begin to find more common interests with other students in his class.

Real and Imagined Losses

A highly respected surgeon once said to me, "If I lose my perfectionism, I'll lose my edge." Many perfectionists identify their perfectionism with all of the personal characteristics that have made them successful in life. Remember the common confusion between perfectionism and striving for excellence. Excellence doesn't mean perfectionism, but rather a combination of talent, energy, and commitment that leads to success. As you and your child move toward freedom from perfectionism, this is an important distinction to keep in mind. You won't be losing your ability to achieve things and do well. If anything, you'll be losing something that may have hampered your success, such as the reluctance to try new things because you were afraid of doing it imperfectly. You can still have the same attentiveness to detail, sense of order, and thoughtfulness that you always had. These characteristics are separate from perfectionism itself. Remember, perfectionism is about what you think you *must* do, not what you actually *can* do.

Still, giving up perfectionism brings a loss of identity as a particular kind of a person. Our personal identity is a focal point for our experience of the world. It's a central part of the way we make sense of things. Changing this can be scary and difficult. The process of freeing your family from perfectionism is a process of building new identities, which is why it isn't achieved overnight.

Make a Note of It

If you've identified perfectionism in yourself, jot down some of the ways this shows up in your life and begin thinking about what it would be like if these things were to disappear. What would you be losing? What would it take to make you more comfortable with this loss? Could some of the things that you do, or some of your personal qualities, still be the same, even if the perfectionism went away?

Talk It Over

Talk with your partner about the roles perfectionism has played in your lives—how each of you, and the whole family, have been affected. As before, this is not done to place blame, but rather to get a better sense of the role of perfectionism in your lives. What effects has it had? Does it offer advantages that would no longer be necessary if the family environment were different? What things would stay the same even if perfectionism disappears?

As your child begins to let go of his perfectionism and talk about new experiences, ask him if he misses anything about the way he used to be. Have any of the changes been scary? Are some ways of behaving hard to give up? Does he see advantages to the way things are now? Is there anything you haven't thought of that might make letting go of his perfectionism easier? Talk often about how your child is doing as things begin to change, and remember to give plenty of encouragement.

Changing the Future

Sometimes when people make big changes for the better in their lives, they realize that things have not been good in the past. It's as though feeling good now highlights how bad things were before. This is a particular kind of loss—a recognition of something that has never been there, rather than a loss of something you had up till now.

We can't change the past, of course. What we can do, though, is learn from the past and begin to do the things that will bring a better future. That's within our power, especially if family members help and support each other. In your family dialogue, remember to acknowledge past difficulties and pains, with an eye toward learning from the past so you can do things differently.

> *If you always do what you always did,*
> *you always get what you always got.*
> —ANONYMOUS

Talk It Over

As you continue to do the family dialogue activities, and when you sense that some progress is being made, talk over any feelings of anger, resentment, or sadness about the way things used to be. Allow time for everyone's feelings to come out. Assure your partner and children that even if these feelings don't come up until sometime later, you'll still be willing to talk about them. They may say something like, "You were always mad at me for the tiniest mistakes," or "You always had some criticism," or "You and Dad always used to fight and yell at each other. It was scary." There may be both sadness and resentment in what they are saying. An attitude of humility and a spirit of cooperation will help in facing this particular kind of grieving.

Remember the goal: you got this far in the process of freeing yourselves from perfectionism through hard work and a commitment to listen to one another and make things better. Whatever happened in the past, the future will be better because of what you're doing right now.

Remember the Gains

For a perfectionist, failure as a human being always seems to be just one mistake away. What a relief it is to be able to shed this fear. Freedom from perfectionism has many advantages, and while it's valuable to be aware of the losses and tend to them, it's also very important to keep the gains clearly in mind.

Psychoanalyst and author Alice Miller described a patient with whom many perfectionists can identify, a woman who frequently had the feeling she was walking on stilts. From her presumably superior perch, she actually envied people who could walk without stilts—who didn't need to impress others and who were, as she movingly described them, "free to be average." What a relief not to be weighted down by constant expectations, not to have to second-guess everything you do or worry endlessly about the impression you're making on others, not to have to stay at the top in everything you do.

Does "free to be average" sound dull? Does it sound like accepting mediocrity? If so, you're looking through the lens of perfectionism. Remember, your capacity for growth, adventure, and enjoyment of life is actually enhanced by having the courage to be imperfect and by leaving behind the constant pressure to meet someone's expectations. Freedom to be average means freedom from having to be the best. That doesn't *keep* you from being the best, it just means you're still acceptable as a person if you're not the best.

If perfectionism has driven you to earn vast sums of money or achieve a spotless home but you're too busy to enjoy life, what does your success mean? Freeing yourself from perfectionism can bring a gain in vitality and the capacity to enjoy life.

Many perfectionists divide their time between critiquing what they did in the past and worrying about how they will do in the future. The net effect is that the present disappears from their experience and time goes faster. One thing you gain from leaving perfectionism behind is that, in a very real sense, you get your life back.

Talk It Over

Talk with your family about what you might all gain by freeing yourselves from perfectionism. Acknowledge whatever regrets or sadness come up as you discuss this. It would be nice to have realized these things earlier, but remind yourselves how fortunate you are to be working on this now, and how bright the future can be. Consider together: what burdens could be lifted by shedding perfectionism?

Take time to enjoy the present. Make a plan to do something fun together, and observe how well you're able to stay in the moment. In other words, notice: Are you paying attention to what's happening moment by moment, or are you thinking about how well you are doing something? Are you worried about past or future problems? Are you worried that you're goofing off or making poor use of your time? Share these thoughts with each other.

Grieving losses, acknowledging pain, anticipating gains, and making plans to move ahead are all part of a process of growth. This process probably won't happen neatly, one step after another, and old feelings will come and go for a while, just as they do in any grieving process. The fears and resentments that surface are best dealt with in an environment where everyone feels emotionally connected and increasingly secure, and where you can focus on making healthy changes. You've been creating this environment by following the suggestions in this book, so you're on the right track. Keep it up.

Chapter 11

Making a Plan Together

Throughout this book, the "Make a Note of It" and "Talk It Over" activities have been aimed at creating a more encouraging, accepting environment in your home. With this as a base, you have begun to look at the ways perfectionism came into your family and at some ways to let go of it. Congratulations on the progress you have made thus far.

Staying with It for the Long Haul

If you've noticed that it's become easier for family members to talk about things, or that you have a greater spirit of cooperation, or that family members feel better about themselves, then you're headed in the right direction. This probably didn't happen overnight. Don't be discouraged if it's taken a while and if you haven't moved as far as you'd like in the process of freeing your family from perfectionism. Family members may be busy with their lives, interest comes and goes, and some family members may even be angry and think your interest in doing this is, in a word, crazy. It's not unusual for things to change slowly, even if you've done all the activities. Keep at it. Simply shaking up the family routine opens the door for further growth.

> *Little strokes fell great oaks.*
> —BENJAMIN FRANKLIN

As a parent, there will be times when you can suggest that the perfectionists in the family might try doing things in a less perfectionist way. In this chapter, you'll get some ideas about intervening directly in perfectionist behaviors and thoughts. The other person is more likely to agree and you're more likely to succeed if the family environment is encouraging.

There's a paradox here that often makes a first attempt to help someone with her perfectionism fall flat. Our usual inclination is to say to the perfectionist, "Oh, you don't always have to be perfect, you know," or "Why don't you just leave it the way it is," or even "Why don't you just make a mistake on purpose so you can see that you'll survive it." The problem with all these comments is not that they're bad advice, it's that the first thought the perfectionist has is that she's done something wrong: *if you criticize me for my perfectionism, it means I haven't been a good enough perfectionist.*

If you've had this frustrating experience, remember to use I-messages. (Try "This is frustrating, and I get scared I won't be able to help you" rather than "Look, just try this and see what happens—what can you lose?") Then ask if your child would be willing to experiment with some ways of reducing tension and being less hard on herself. Children will usually want to do this, it's just that change is scary.

Responding to Mistakes

In the spirit of openness within the family, try modeling a new attitude about your own mistakes. By talking about mistakes you've made, large or small, and apologizing for them if they've had a direct effect on your child, you can signal that being imperfect is safe in your home.

Talk It Over

During a time of family dialogue, after you've established a level of comfort with these discussions, have a conversation about mistakes. What does everyone think about making a mistake: Is it embarrassing or is it okay? Does anyone feel criticized for mistakes? Are there people outside the family (teachers, classmates, bosses, coaches) who seem overly critical of mistakes? Does anyone feel they should absolutely never make a mistake? If other family members think you have been supercritical, acknowledge this and talk about what you'd like to do differently.

Make a plan for how to respond in your day-to-day family life when someone makes self-critical comments. If your child says, "I'm so stupid," it's helpful to ask if he's feeling bad about himself right then, or embarrassed, or discouraged. Leave it at that, rather than saying, "No, you aren't stupid." He isn't, of course, but remember these are expressions of discouragement more than statements of fact.

Reactions such as "This is great, except for . . . " and "You did a great job, but . . . " give something and take it away in the same breath. Say what you truly like about the job or the situation and save the critique for another time.

Become aware of the times when you do something for your children that they could do for themselves. Even young children want to be helpful and cooperative if given the chance. Parents of young Montessori students are regularly thrilled to have their children cleaning up tabletops the way they learned to do in school. Of course you want to help your child get things done well, and sometimes things do need to be done in a hurry (sadly), but remember that the message to your child may be, "You can't do this well enough to suit me." Whenever possible, all the way from younger children getting dressed to older ones meeting obligations at school or in extra-curricular activities, allow your children to assume responsibilities and give them plenty of encouragement when they do.

Based on what you've learned about where perfectionism comes from in your particular family, how it shows up, and how responsive your children might be, make a plan with your partner for ways to reduce perfectionism. Jot down some things you can say or do that you think would be helpful, and talk about which of you will do what. Then put the ideas into practice. Check in with each other regularly—every day for a while, then at least every week—to see how it's going. Modify the plan as needed. Stay on track by consulting and modifying your notes.

Plans for Your Child

Ask your children to do some specific things as well in the effort to move toward overcoming perfectionism. Make a plan with your child to do some of these. Do them together if appropriate, or have your child do them and check in with him later to see how he's doing.

A Plan for Beginnings

Perfectionists often have trouble getting started. The thought of being judged weighs heavily against doing a project at all, and the prospect of having to get the job done exactly right quickly becomes overwhelming. With these apprehensions in mind, take a cue from the one day at a time approach used in addiction recovery programs. Suggest to your child—or your partner, or yourself—that doing some *small piece* of a project and then taking a break might be helpful. That takes the focus away from how huge and overwhelming the whole project is.

Which piece is the right one to start with? Any one will usually do. Start with some part of the project that seems most interesting. This can kindle interest in the rest, which keeps the momentum going.

If your child is willing to try the small-piece approach, be nearby for support and encouragement. Make a plan to do this for several projects in a row. School projects, thank-you letters, room cleaning, and any other task that has a beginning and an end are fair game.

Chou and Susan had worked hard with their family to create an ongoing dialogue and find ways to be more aware of each other's feelings. They committed themselves, in the midst of busy lives, to having a fun night each week, rotating which family member would choose the activity. All of this had helped create the right kind of environment for Chou to help Allan, their 12-year-old, with the way Allan was pressuring himself.

Allan usually sat down to do his homework in the evening and became more and more distressed, finally giving up and yelling that he was "a stupid idiot." Chou decided he would devote some time to working with Allan. They sat together in the den. Chou brought some of his own work, and he and Allan started by talking about Allan's day or whatever came up, and then Chou would say, "Okay, work time. Let me know if you need something." If Allan started to become agitated, Chou asked if he had any questions. If he did, Chou discussed whatever the problem was. If not, Chou talked with him in a casual way about something for a few minutes, and then said, "Okay, work time again."

The extra attention and Chou's relaxed manner while doing his own work eventually helped Allan to become less agitated and less hard on himself. At the end of a session, Chou would say, "Okay, time to pack it in," and they went off to join the rest of the family for a snack.

A Plan for Endings

Some perfectionists have trouble completing projects. The project may be done, but is it done right? Is it perfect? Isn't there just one more thing, or maybe two, that should be done?

In many cases, it's helpful to set a goal of completing what's required, checking it over, and considering it done. Have a ceremony when it's finished, and either take a break or move on to something interesting. Make a plan with your child to do this, and join in the ceremony.

I'd like to pass along some lessons I've learned about endings and perfectionism from my own experience with writing this book. Letting go of projects without becoming obsessed with minor details may become easier for me now. I've learned that no matter how perfect I think some of my writing is, my helpful editor is there to suggest ways to make it even better. The lesson for me is not that I can't write. I've learned that opinions vary on what's appropriate, that this depends in part on who my audience is, and that although good writing is a possibility, perfect writing is an illusion. As a result of what I've learned, I'm hoping to become better in other areas of my life at offering what I have to offer and letting it go at that, period.

A Plan for Making Decisions

Perfectionists often have trouble making decisions. Putting your money on one side or the other means you are committed to a choice that could turn out to be wrong, or less satisfying than other choices. The fear of making a mistake leads to indecisiveness and inaction.

Considering the pros and cons, and even writing them down, are important first steps in making a decision about what to do. Help your child do this with a decision she's facing. As you talk together about the options and what she thinks of each one, you may be able to hear what her attitudes are. Is your child particularly animated about some of the pros for one of the options? Is she highly distressed by some of the cons? Tell her what you're noticing without pressing your own view.

■ "You seem to be heading in a particular direction with this . . . [name it]. How does this feel?"

■ "It sounds like you just can't stand the thought of that happening. Does that make this option out of the question for you?"

Perfectionists may have several concerns when faced with a decision: What do other people want me to do? What if a particular choice puts me on one side of an issue and some people are displeased? What if it turns out that the other choice would have been better? Do I know enough to decide?

All of these concerns are legitimate, but any of them can bog a perfectionist down. Since the consequences of a particular choice can be a prime consideration, it often helps to ask, "What's the worst that can happen?" After getting beyond the usual extremes such as "I'll end up penniless and alone" and "Everyone on the planet will totally hate me and never want to see me again," look at the major realistic concerns and ask what might be done about them. Making a plan for a worst-case scenario often makes other concerns easier to handle.

A related approach is to select what seems best and plan for the consequences of that choice. Most choices have a downside, but you can often build into your decision specific ways to cope with them.

Once a decision is made, it helps to commit yourself to your choice and leave the concerns behind. Perfectionists are great at second-guessing themselves—"What if I forgot about something?"—so planning to march ahead once a decision is made is a good idea.

Make a plan with your child to carry through on a particular choice she has had to make, and check to see how it goes for a period of time. Talk about the concerns that made choosing difficult and remember to affirm your child's growing ability to make choices and go on with life.

Many men go fishing all of their lives
without knowing that it is not fish they are after.
—HENRY DAVID THOREAU

A Plan for Challenging Perfectionistic Expressions

If your child struggles with many of the perfectionistic thoughts you read about in Chapter 1 (pages 7–23), you can make a plan with your child to challenge them. If he often says, "I'm really stupid," have a conversation, when things are going well, about whether he really thinks he's stupid. Tell him what you think about that as well. Let him know you're concerned about him putting himself down, and ask if he would be willing to challenge that. Right after he says he's stupid, he might agree to say, "No, I'm not stupid, I just made a mistake." If he doesn't say it, you might gently remind him: "Isn't this just one of those mistakes?"

It's also important to ask, "Who says you aren't good enough?" or, "Who says you have to be perfect?" The usual expectation, though, when we ask such a question, is that the perfectionist will say something like, "Well, I guess no one says. Wow, I guess that means I can stop being a perfectionist." We wish it was that simple! The belief that people are judging us is deep, and a perfectionist family environment may be contributing to it. Most often, a perfectionist will say, "It's just me—I'm the one who is hard on myself all the time," and then feel discouraged for being all the more imperfect. Everyone ends up puzzled about why a child would do this to himself.

Challenge the idea anyway. Ask your child (this is more likely to be appropriate for older children, who can wrestle with abstractions better) to think about where the idea comes from, including the possibility that it comes from you or your partner. If you've discussed this before, this time, ask your child to challenge his belief and to begin thinking about whether anyone actually wants him to be perfect. This question, by itself, won't cause him to drop his perfectionism, but it's an important part of the process.

A Plan that Supports Problem Solving

Any of the suggestions given here will work better in an environment of acceptance and encouragement. It's all too easy for a child who doesn't feel acceptable to hear any idea about changing, no matter how good it might be, as a criticism of how she's doing things now and to feel more discouraged as a result. This will undermine even the best approaches to change.

When you and your child make a plan to do something differently, the primary goal is not so much to show her a better way, but to do something cooperatively with her to solve a problem. The message in this is that she's important to you, that you want to be patient and not critical, and that if one attempt to solve the problem doesn't work, you'll help her look for another. This attitude will make it easier for her to try new things, and the many good ideas for making changes will have a better chance of working. There are many ways to solve problems when we believe in ourselves, and when we believe that others believe in us.

 Read More About It

These books have excellent exercises to work into your ongoing plan. Choose ones that fit for your particular family. Each includes evaluation tools to help you learn more about your own or your children's perfectionist tendencies.

Never Good Enough: How to Use Perfectionism to Your Advantage Without Letting it Ruin Your Life by Monica R. Basco (New York: Simon & Schuster, 2000). This book gives many examples of ways to handle specific perfectionist thoughts and behaviors.

Too Perfect: When Being in Control Gets Out of Control by Allan E. Mallinger and Jeannette DeWyze (New York: Clarkson Potter, 1992). This book contains numerous useful exercises you might wish to include in your plan. It points out the relationship issues in overcoming perfectionism and explores the role of self-understanding.

Especially for Young Children

Here are a few books that can be read to young children. Their message is that you are lovable—and perfect—just as you are. Think about this for yourself.

Anthony, The Perfect Monster by Angelo DeCesare (New York: Random House, Beginner Books, 1996).

Liking Myself by Pat Palmer (San Luis Obispo, CA: Impact Publishers, 1977).

Persnickity by Stephen Cosgrove (New York: Price Stern Sloan, 1988).

Closing the Book on Perfectionism

Congratulations to you for taking the time to read this book and for taking steps to help free your family from perfectionism. Celebrate any insights you've gained and any progress you've made as you've worked on the suggested activities. Over the months and years ahead, keep revisiting your plans as often as necessary. The approach you've undertaken is one that aims at improving understanding and emotional connections among family members. It's useful even if there is no perfectionism to be concerned about, and for perfectionists it's the way to greater security and self-acceptance. You may not be there yet, but you're on your way.

If you're concerned that you haven't perfectly stamped out perfectionism in your family, try meditating on the Serenity Prayer, written by Reinhold Niebuhr. The best known part of it is, "God grant me the serenity to accept the things I cannot change, the courage to change the things I can, and the wisdom to know the difference."

Let me close by offering you four bits of wisdom that have been helpful to the many families I've worked with in my counseling practice over the years. May they make your road to change a little smoother.

You May Not Have Heard the Last of It

Because perfectionism is so much a part of you or your child, it may never entirely disappear. Instead, you may simply see it from a greater distance. You will begin to recognize when it comes up, and you'll be able to say, "There's my perfectionism again." This emotional distance allows you to become disentangled from the perfectionism, even if it's still there in some ways.

As a recovering perfectionist myself, I've often told people that I've never quit smoking. Saying "I've quit" is too definite—it could prove wrong, after all. Instead, I'm just seeing how long I can go without a cigarette. As this book is being written, it's been 36 years.

There's my perfectionism again—okay, I've quit. But even after all this time, it still seems hard to say that, especially in print.

Consider an Attitude Adjustment

When you work on overcoming a troubling set of behaviors, it's easy to get into a self-deprivation mode. You might think you have to make yourself abstain from the behavior and learn to do without it. I suggest a self-care approach instead, in which you view behavior changes as part of an overall pattern of increasing wellness. Your attitude about what you're doing is the important thing. Freeing your family from perfectionism is best done when the intention is the overall emotional growth of the family, rather than getting rid of an objectionable behavior, which only intensifies perfectionism.

Expect Progress, Not Perfection

It's normal to have good and bad days in this process. Change in the family's emotional atmosphere rarely runs in a straight line from where you are to where you want to be. It's more like a spiral. If something doesn't go well, you may think you've circled back to where you began, but you're probably on a higher level of the spiral. Small differences in how people treat one another and a growing ability to solve problems together all add up. Keep at it.

Imperfection Is Interesting

People will never be perfect. That's part of what makes for problems in the world, but it's also part of what makes the world interesting. It's important that we all work for a better world, but working for perfection only leads to overwork and constant dissatisfaction. The psychiatrist W.L. "Bill" Pew used to give every client he worked with the same diagnosis: Chronic Human Imperfection. I like that attitude.

What, after all, is a halo? It's only one more thing to keep clean.
—Christopher Fry

Bibliography

Books and Periodicals

Adderholdt, Miriam and Jan Goldberg. *Perfectionism: What's Bad About Being Too Good?* Revised and updated edition. Minneapolis: Free Spirit Publishing, 1999.

Basco, Monica R. *Never Good Enough: How to Use Perfectionism to Your Advantage Without Letting it Ruin Your Life.* New York: Simon & Schuster, 2000.

Burns, David D. "The Perfectionist's Script for Self-Defeat." *Psychology Today* 14, no. 6 (1980): 34–52.

Cosgrove, Stephen. *Persnickity.* New York: Price Stern Sloan, 1988.

DeCesare, Angelo. *Anthony, the Perfect Monster.* New York: Random House, Beginner Books, 1996.

Dinkmeyer, Don C., and Gary D. McKay. *Raising a Responsible Child: How to Prepare Your Child for Today's Complex World.* New York: Fireside, 1996.

Doherty, William J. *Take Back Your Kids: Confident Parenting in Turbulent Times.* Notre Dame, IN: Sorin Books, 2000.

Frost, Randy, Patricia Marten, Cathleen Lahart, and Robin Rosenblate. "The Dimensions of Perfectionism." *Cognitive Therapy and Research* 14, no. 5 (1990): 449–468.

Galbraith, Judy and Jim Delisle. *The Gifted Kids' Survival Guide: A Teen Handbook.* Minneapolis: Free Spirit Publishing, 1996.

Greenspon, Thomas S. "'Healthy Perfectionism' Is an Oxymoron! Reflections on the Psychology of Perfectionism and the Sociology of Science," *The Journal of Secondary Gifted Education* XI (2000): 197–208.

Hewitt, Paul and Gordon Flett. "Perfectionism in the Self and Social Contexts: Conceptualization, Assessment, and Association with Psychopathology." *Journal of Personality and Social Psychology* 60, no. 3 (1991): 456–470.

Hipp, Earl. *Fighting Invisible Tigers*. Minneapolis, Free Spirit Publishing, 1995.

Kohn, Alfie. *Punished by Rewards: The Trouble with Gold Stars, Incentive Plans, A's, Praise, and Other Bribes*. Boston: Houghton Mifflin, 1999.

Lerner, Harriet. *The Dance of Anger: A Woman's Guide to Changing the Patterns of Intimate Relationships*. New York: HarperCollins, 1997.

Mallinger, Allan E., and Jeannette DeWyze. *Too Perfect: When Being in Control Gets Out of Control*. New York: Clarkson Potter, 1992.

Terner, Janet and William L. Pew. *The Courage to Be Imperfect: The Life and Work of Rudolf Dreikurs*. New York: Hawthorn Books, 1978.

Walsh, David. *Selling Out America's Children: How America Puts Profits before Values—and What Parents Can Do*. Minneapolis: Fairview Press, 1995.

Online University Counseling Center Brochures

Perfectionism
Counseling Center, University of Illinois at Champaign-Urbana
www.couns.uiuc.edu/Brochures/perfecti.htm

Perfectionism: A Double-Edged Sword
Counseling and Mental Health Center, University of Texas at Austin
www.utexas.edu/student/cmhc/booklets/perfection/perfect.html

Web site

The Anna Westin Foundation
www.annawestinfoundation.org

Notes

Notes

Index

About the Author

Tom Greenspon is a Licensed Psychologist and Licensed Marriage and Family Therapist in private practice in Minneapolis, Minnesota. He earned a B.A. from Yale and a Ph.D. in psychology from the University of Illinois in 1968. After a postdoctoral fellowship at the University of Rochester, New York, he joined the faculty of the Medical Center at the University of Alabama in Birmingham. He moved to the Twin Cities in 1977.

Tom lectures and writes on a variety of topics, including the emotional needs of gifted children and adults. He is a member of several professional organizations, has authored a monograph on adolescent-adult relationships for the Unitarian Universalist Association, and has recently published articles about perfectionism and the self-experience of gifted individuals. He provides clinical supervision in psychodynamic psychotherapy.

Tom is married to Barbara C. Greenspon, M.A., his partner in private practice. They cofounded the Childbirth Education Association of Greater Birmingham, were advisors to Unitarian Universalist youth groups on local and national levels, and have cotaught courses on human sexuality. Both are certified as sex counselors and educators.

Tom and Barbara are former copresidents of the Minnesota Council for the Gifted and Talented and served on the Minnesota State Advisory Committee for Gifted. Tom is the recipient of the 1998 MCGT Award for Distinguished Service to Gifted Individuals.

Other Great Books from Free Spirit

Perfectionism
What's Bad About Being Too Good?
Revised and Updated Edition
by Miriam Adderholdt, Ph.D., and Jan Goldberg
This revised and updated edition includes new research and statistics on the causes and consequences of perfectionism, biographical sketches of famous perfectionists and risk takers, and resources for readers who want to know more. For ages 13 & up.
$12.95; 136 pp.; softcover; illus.; 6" x 9"

How to Handle a Hard-to-Handle Kid
A Parents' Guide to Understanding and Changing Problem Behaviors
by C. Drew Edwards, Ph.D.
Packed with practical information and real-life examples, written with authority and compassion, this is a book you'll turn to often for advice, insight, and more on parenting a high-maintenance child. These strategies really work. For parents of children ages 3–12.
$15.95; 232 pp.; softcover; illus.; 6" x 9"

Fighting Invisible Tigers
A Stress Management Guide for Teens
Revised & Updated
by Earl Hipp
Proven, practical advice for teens on coping with stress, being assertive, building relationships, taking risks, making decisions, dealing with fears, and more. For ages 11 & up.
$12.95; 160 pp.; softcover; illus.; 6" x 9"

Leader's Guide
12 Sessions on Stress Management and Lifeskills Development
by Connie C. Schmitz, Ph.D., with Earl Hipp
For grades 6–12.
$19.95; 136 pp.; softcover; 8½" x 11"

The Gifted Kids' Survival Guide

For Ages 10 & Under
Revised & Updated Edition
by Judy Galbraith, M.A.
First published in 1984, newly revised and updated, this book has helped countless young gifted children realize they're not alone, they're not "weird," and being smart, talented, and creative is a bonus, not a burden. Includes advice from hundreds of gifted kids. For ages 10 & under.
$9.95; 104 pp.; softcover; illus.; 6" x 9"

The Gifted Kids' Survival Guide

A Teen Handbook
Revised, Expanded, and Updated Edition
by Judy Galbraith, M.A., and Jim Delisle, Ph.D.
Vital information on giftedness, IQ, school success, college planning, stress, perfectionism, and much more. For ages 11–18.
$15.95; 304 pp.; softcover; illus.; 7¼" x 9¼"

When Nothing Matters Anymore

A Survival Guide for Depressed Teens
by Bev Cobain, R.N.,C.
Written for teens with depression—and those who feel despondent, dejected, or alone—this powerful book offers help, hope, and potentially life-saving facts and advice. Includes true stories from teens who have dealt with depression, survival tips, resources, and more. For ages 13 & up.
$13.95; 176 pp.; softcover; illus.; 6" x 9"

To place an order or to request a free catalog of SELF–HELP FOR KIDS® and SELF–HELP FOR TEENS® materials, please write, call, email, or visit our Web site:

Free Spirit Publishing Inc.
217 Fifth Avenue North • Suite 200 • Minneapolis, MN 55401-1299
toll-free 800.735.7323 • local 612.338.2068 • fax 612.337.5050
help4kids@freespirit.com • www.freespirit.com

Visit us on the Web!

www.freespirit.com

Stop by anytime to find our Parents' Choice Approved catalog with fast, easy, secure 24-hour online ordering; "Ask Our Authors," where visitors ask questions—and authors give answers—on topics important to children, teens, parents, teachers, and others who care about kids; links to other Web sites we know and recommend; fun stuff for everyone, including quick tips and strategies from our books; and much more! Plus our site is completely searchable so you can find what you need in a hurry. Stop in and let us know what you think!

Just point and click!

 Get the first look at our books, catch the latest news from Free Spirit, and check out our site's newest features.

 Do you have a question for us or for one of our authors? Send us an email. Whenever possible, you'll receive a response within 48 hours.

order! Order in confidence! Our secure server uses the most sophisticated online ordering technology available. And ordering online is just one of the ways to purchase our books: you can also order by phone, fax, or regular mail. No matter which method you choose, excellent service is our goal.

1.800.735.7323 • fax 612.337.5050 • help4kids@freespirit.com